Forever Parents

Forever Parents

Adopting Older Children

James E. Kloeppel

and

Darlene A. Kloeppel

Adele Enterprises
Union City, Georgia

To Christopher, Jonathan, Betty, and Thomas:
without whom this book could never have been written.

Copyright © 1995 by James E. Kloeppel

Published by: Adele Enterprises
              PO Box 553
              Union City, GA 30291-0553

Manufactured in the United States of America

Publisher's Cataloging-in-Publication Data

Kloeppel, James E.
    Forever parents: adopting older children/
    James E. Kloeppel, Darlene A. Kloeppel.
        p. cm.
    ISBN 0-9640374-1-6
    1. Adopted children — United States.   2. Parenting —
    United States.
    I. Kloeppel, Darlene A.   II. Title
HV875.K56 1995
362.734

Library of Congress Catalog Card Number: 95-94017

Contents

Preface

Long before Darlene and I met and fell in love, we had a mutual friend. His name was Leslie.

Leslie was our same age, and in most ways, he was just an ordinary kid. Leslie enjoyed sports, did fine in school, and had a good sense of humor. He was well-liked by others, both children and adults. Leslie was responsible, dependable, and fun to be around. But Leslie was also different in a very special way. Leslie was a foster child.

Neither Darlene nor I knew why Leslie had been placed in foster care. He never offered to explain, and we never asked. At the tender age of twelve, Leslie was considered "too old" to be adopted and grew to adulthood in one of his foster homes.

Today, there are many "Leslies" in the world: young boys and girls removed from neglectful or abusive birth parents who grow up without the benefits of a consistent family home. Never adopted, these children are deprived of a mother or father willing to share a lifetime of their love, their lives, and their name. No permanent parents exist with whom the children can share celebrations such as Father's Day or Mother's Day. They have no place to truly call "home." Despite the love and nurturing offered by the foster care system, a fundamental difference between foster parents and adoptive parents remains. Foster parents are meant to be temporary parents, but adoptive parents become a child's *forever parents.*

For many years, adoption agencies were unable to place older children in adoptive homes. The reason: most people wanted infants and simply would not accept older children. Older children bring a history of experiences and learned behaviors, many of which are destructive and inappropriate in a stable, nurturing living environment. Most potential parents did not believe that feelings or behaviors caused by insecurity, low self-worth, and poor treatment could ever be altered, or that children could ever be "normal" if they had experienced rejection, neglect, or abuse in their early years of life. Indeed, these are big obstacles to overcome. Fortunately, the tide of opinion is turning. More people are now willing to consider adopting an older child.

Twelve years into our marriage, Darlene and I decided to adopt older children. Christopher (age 5) and Jonathan (age 4) entered our home and our lives in December of 1987. Despite our preparation and good intentions, the first six months of adjustment were horrible, far worse than we had ever imagined. At times we wondered whether it would work out. But progress was gradually made, and the adoption was successful. So successful, in fact, that several years later we decided to adopt again. Betty (age 9) and Thomas (age 7) arrived in December of 1991.

The first six months were again horrible — worse than we had anticipated, even with our previous experience. Forget progress; simply surviving those first six months became a goal unto itself. As we experienced the tough times with Betty and Thomas, we saw a pattern unfold. History seemed to be repeating itself as the children's emotions erupted into our lives. The same destructive behaviors and uncontrollable emotional outbursts occurred a second time, as our relationship with our new children grew and matured. We persevered, partly because we knew from experience that it could work. The going would be rough, but eventually we would emerge as a family. Though difficult to tolerate, such initial angry and disruptive feelings and behavior are normal, essential to the children's development. Eventually, however, commitment and persistence result in progress, and the relationship begins to grow more positively.

Some of our parenting experiences are known to all families with children, adopted or not. We share some similarities with step-families, where half-grown children are thrust into new family relationships, after what may have been a difficult series of family problems. Some of our situations we hold in common with families who have adopted infants. But, some of the problems we encountered were unique in that we had adopted older children.

Many people have misconceptions about what it is like to adopt an older child or to be adopted as a child. Some tend to idealize the adoptive parents thinking, "Aren't those people so wonderful!" or "It's such a nice thing you are doing." Others feel a certain stigma attached to adoptive children — that despite all efforts the children are going to turn out to be just terrible, horrible, awful kids.

We believe it would be helpful for other people to see the

reality of adoption — that kids have had difficult experiences, they go into a new family situation, there are tough times, there are good times, relationships are formed, and the kids grow up. *Forever Parents* is not intended to serve as a practical guide for the adoptive parent. It is, rather, the story of what one family experienced through the adoption process — not once, but twice. It is the story of people, learning to live with and love one another through the creation of a family. It is the story of the many problems, pitfalls, and blessings of learning to adopt and adapt.

There are no paragons of virtue about to be revealed on these pages. Simply normal, everyday people who cope, cry, and grow frustrated like you and anyone else, though for a while, perhaps, much more than usual. We can write these pages now because the major adjustments are behind us...we hope.

This book is a compilation of our experiences with adopting older children. Our children came to us having received few opportunities for achieving their potential. They were little people whose personalities were partly formed, with definite likes and dislikes, and the fully formed voices to air them. How this process of our adoption of them and their adoption of us affected our lives is the object of our story.

Adoptive children need love, understanding, and support. Likewise, adoptive parents need love, understanding, and above all else, support through the difficult days following the placement of a child in their home. *Forever Parents* is intended for prospective adoptive parents, for their family and friends, and for the general public, that all might better understand and appreciate the many trials and tribulations which must be met and overcome along the road of adoption.

Forever Parents is about children and parents who have waited their turns in the lengthy adoption process, and despite outward appearances at times, desperately want it to work. We hope our story encourages others to consider adopting older children into their lives.

Chapter One

How It All Began

Darlene took the car and the television. I kept the stereo and the microwave. She left early on a Monday morning. By the evening of that first day we were 500 miles apart. The following day the gap had widened to well over a thousand miles. Surprisingly, this distance seemed small compared to the rift which had recently grown between us.

Six months earlier I had learned — quite by accident — that I was unable to have children. The discovery had come easily, but acceptance was a long way off.

I had been seeing a doctor concerning a strange infection in my kidneys, bladder, and prostate. One of the routine tests the doctor had performed was a sperm count. I remember his phone call as though it were yesterday.

I was working in my office at the observatory on the University of Colorado campus when the telephone rang.

"Mr. Kloeppel, this is Dr. _____," said the voice on the other end. "I'm referring you to a specialist."

"Wh...why, ...wh...what for?" I stammered, thinking I was about to die from some deadly disease.

"Well, because you can't have kids," came the doctor's quick and tactless response. He might as well have stuck me through the heart with a hypodermic needle.

"You have an extremely low sperm count," he impassively continued. "And of the few sperm you *are* producing, almost all are deformed with very low motility and mobility. You need to see a specialist."

I was stunned. I didn't know what the words "very low motility and mobility" meant, but I knew it wasn't good. *I couldn't have kids?* I was shocked. No, I was more than shocked. I was devastated. I numbly hung up the phone, quietly left my office, and slowly climbed the steps to the observatory's dome. There, I stepped outside on the catwalk where, out of sight from anyone, I sat down and cried.

I cried for a long time.

Feelings I never knew I possessed surged from deep within my heart and soul and poured from my eyes. Just moments before, I had briefly feared my own death. Now I was suddenly grieving the deaths of my unborn children. I was terribly saddened and bitterly disappointed.

I took the rest of the day off. I swung by the doctor's office on my way home to pick up the test results and referral form, and filled my prescription at a nearby liquor store — a six-pack of Henry Weinhard's Private Reserve. Then I went home, broke open the six-pack, and broke the news to Darlene.

She took the news fairly well. While she was very sad and greatly disappointed, she was not totally surprised. After all, we had been married for seven years, often doing what married people often do. But our efforts had never produced a child. Now we knew they never would.

After we sobbed together for awhile, Darlene spoke in a quiet, reassuring tone. She told me that she still loved me. She told me that, even if I couldn't have children, I was still a man. And, hoping to raise my hope, she suggested that maybe the doctor's initial prognosis was wrong. We would soon find out.

The specialist was kind and considerate. The tests were quick and conclusive. I learned I had a congenital birth defect. Could I have kids? No. Was there anything the specialist, or anybody else, could do? No. I was sterile and could not have children — not now, not ever — and that was all there was to it. Period. End of discussion.

I accepted the final verdict with very little emotion. I guess I had really known deep down there was very little hope. I had already grieved the loss of a life I would never know. But, while I could not have children, there was no reason to suspect that Darlene could not. I did the only decent thing I could think of at the time. I offered Darlene her freedom through divorce.

Fortunately for me, she did not accept the offer. It could have been the biggest mistake of my life.

*****

The conversation had started as one of those excited discussions that engaged couples often have about their future lives together. The issue of suitable housing was raised, and the question of how many children we planned to house followed naturally.

"We'll have two of our own and adopt twenty!" My half-serious, half-joking reply to his question startled my husband-to-be into thoughtful consideration of our compatibility.

"Are you crazy?!" he responded. "We couldn't possibly have that many kids!" He sat down and stared at me.

I was nineteen, I was studying to be a social worker, and I didn't see why we couldn't have that many children. In what was my characteristic fashion when confronted by the suggestion that an idea is impossible, I began to present philosophically all the reasons why a family of 22 natural-born and adopted children was a possible and even a reasonable option. My arguments ranged from purely theoretical (raising 22 children can't be that terrible — people in other countries often have much larger families than Americans) to environmentally conscious (it is socially irresponsible to bring more than two children into an already overcrowded world — adopting most of them would make more sense) to personal (as a social worker, I would be trained to understand and help children with problems who otherwise might not have a loving family).

My counterpart, in his characteristic fashion when confronted by a totally unexpected and unconventional idea for the first time, began to point out all the reasons why a family of 22 natural-born and adopted children was a bizarre and unworkable possibility. His arguments ranged from theoretical (wanting a family was different than running a group home for orphans) to financial (supporting a family of 24 people meant we would have to earn an incredible amount of money, since neither of us would inherit a fortune in the near future) to personal (people would think we were weird — he would think we were weird!).

Financial practicality finally overtook my philosophical

*argument, and we decided agreeably on having "some chil-
dren," postponing the decision about how many to have until
we completed college. We married and moved into a mobile
home, I took birth control pills and the subject of children
did not re-surface for several years.*

* * * * *

The next six months were extremely difficult for me, for
Darlene, and for our relationship. I resented my situation,
feared that Darlene resented hers, and became very de-
pressed as a result of both. I felt like I was no longer "me,"
that I had suddenly become someone else — and I didn't
like that other person. I started drinking too much. I started
smoking again. Darlene cautiously suggested that maybe I
should see a counselor, but I refused. "I'm not *nuts*," I
protested. "I'm *sterile!*"

As the only man-child of my father's family, I had long
felt compelled, expected, even obligated to carry on the
family name. You know, blood-of-my-blood, bones-of-my-
bones, that sort of thing. But on our family tree, the Jim limb
had been broken off. There would be no buds — no little
Kloeppels to carry on the family lineage. My feelings of self-
worth plummeted to an all-time low. I felt so guilty and
ashamed.

Darlene thoughtfully offered to tell our family and friends
that it was she who could not have children, but I couldn't let
her do that. This was my burden to bear, and I felt compelled
to bear it alone. As a result, the rift between Darlene and me
widened.

How *would* my parents and two older sisters react to my dreadful news? How would my friends feel? Would I still be loved and accepted under these terrible new terms? For my own peace of mind, I had to find out, and fast.

First, we told our friends in Colorado. Then we drove to Arizona to tell our friends there. Then we traveled to Nebraska to tell other friends. And, finally, the worse trip of all. We journeyed to Iowa to tell our families.

Predictably, reactions varied from "So what?" to "Gee, that's too bad...you would have made such fine parents." Unpredictably, no one — not a single person — thought I was a low-life because I could not sire children. My worst fear had not materialized. Yes, my family and most of my friends were disappointed, but they still loved and accepted me. This knowledge and security ultimately helped me over the terrible hump.

Looking back, I now realize that the physical handicap of being sterile also loomed large as both a mental and an emotional handicap in my life. Deep down, I guess I knew that I would eventually get over it — even come to accept it — and life would go on. But that amorphous "gut feeling" sure didn't help at the time.

I spent many long hours at the observatory, making up work to do, to avoid being around Darlene. I hiked alone in the mountains, exploring old mines and ghost towns. In reality, I wasn't so much searching for the past as much as I was seeking a new direction for the future. I'm afraid I wasn't much of a husband, friend, or companion for quite some time.

On top of our personal problems, Darlene's career aspirations in Colorado had not worked out especially well. With an ulterior motive in mind, I encouraged her to look for a job elsewhere. She did, was offered several, and accepted a position in Atlanta, Georgia.

So, on that cold morning in February, Darlene left for a new job and a new life in Atlanta. Little did she realize that I had no intention of joining her.

* * * * *

We had purchased a house in Arizona and decided it was time to start a family. I quit taking birth control pills, and we waited. Months passed and we still waited. (Well, we did a few things besides wait, but to no avail.) Jim took a job in Colorado, so we moved and kept trying. I took my temperature, I had dreams of being pregnant, I prayed—but each month we were disappointed again. The uneasy feeling that something might be wrong hovered uncomfortably close. But it was unthinkable. We did not discuss it; we merely waited.

Jim developed a kidney infection and, during related treatment, supplied the doctor with a semen specimen. Totally devoid of compassion, the doctor simply informed Jim that he would be incapable of fathering children. Stunned, Jim did have the presence of mind to get a referral to a fertility specialist and then came home devastated.

He would not let me accompany him to see the specialist. Although a more humanitarian exchange took place, the results were basically the same. I tried to say what I could to help Jim deal with the news. It really did not matter to me. We could adopt kids if we wanted some. But Jim would have none of it. He withdrew further and further, struggling alone with his identity as a man and a husband. We went through a period when Jim needed to tell everyone he knew that he was sterile, mostly to see their reactions, and then we didn't talk about it anymore.

* * * * *

Nearly five months later I finally came to my senses. I left my job, packed my belongings, and joined Darlene in Georgia. There I assumed a lifestyle much like that portrayed in the old "Grizzly Adams" television series. I buried myself in rebuilding an old farm house, cutting down trees and splitting them into firewood, clearing the land, and gardening (well, actually Darlene did most of the gardening).

The new start was refreshing. Though I didn't realize it at the time, the move — abandoning my old life and beginning a new life in Georgia — was instrumental to my being healed both mentally and emotionally. Such major changes may not be required for everyone in similar circumstances, but they were clearly essential for me.

No one in Atlanta knew my little "secret," and at first I didn't feel particularly compelled to tell anyone. The old pangs of disappointment, regret, and fear still bubbled to the surface occasionally, but I could now deal with them more effectively. At last, I felt like my burden was finally being lifted.

I made a number of good friends in the Deep South. As my friendships deepened, I chose to tell a few of my closest friends that I could not have children. Several of them asked if Darlene and I had considered adoption. As a matter of fact, Darlene had. I had not.

In September of 1982, Darlene had written the following note in her diary: "I am really okay with not having kids. I really see no difference between adopting and having your own, except that I will never have the experience of carrying a child. I have mixed feelings about that anyway. Jim doesn't want to adopt though."

For me, adoption was wholly, completely, unequivocally out of the question. To create a family biologically was one thing; to create one legally was another matter entirely. To my mind's eye, adopted children were different. Adopted children were...well, there was something *wrong* with them. Why should I adopt someone else's problem?

Adoption was clearly risky business. If I adopted, whose child would I get? What would the child be like? What would the child's parents be like? Would the child have health problems? Physical problems? Mental problems? Or, horror of horrors, *emotional* problems?

Would an adopted child be accepted as mine by my family? By friends? By strangers? By the child? By *me*? Would I — indeed, could I — learn to love the child? Would he or she learn to love me?

And there were the more practical questions. Would I be a good father? Would Darlene be a good mother? *Would it work?*

In years past, I have occasionally prided myself in my excellent ability to rationalize my way out of unpleasant and somewhat sticky situations. In this instance, I rose fabulously to the occasion. We were too busy. We couldn't afford a family. Our house wasn't big enough. We had been married seemingly forever (why risk disturbing that?). And lastly, my biggest and best rationalization of all: *If God had wanted me to have children, he would not have made me sterile.*

With so many concerns, fears, questions, and prized rationalizations, it was much easier for me to just shove the whole matter aside and forget about it. I dug my heels in and adamantly refused to consider the subject further.

* * * * *

Building a house had been our primary concern for the past several years. Jim and I had spent almost all of our available time repairing, expanding, and renovating —transforming a tiny 4-room ramshackle shell into a 3-bedroom custom-designed home. The majority of the project was complete, and Jim had taken a job that required out-of-state travel for several months at a time. After work, I continued to fill my evenings and weekends with activities to finish the house. Some construction tasks (like planning, measuring, and cutting) required that I pay close attention to what I was doing, but others (like brushing three coats of varnish on a wall) allowed my mind to wander to realms far from the task at hand. It was during those long hours of unstructured daydreaming that I again began to think about a family.

In retrospect, the thought did not seem quite so random. After all, we had directed a considerable amount of effort toward building a "nest," and we had chosen (for reasons quite unrelated to having children, we thought) to build a family-sized home instead of a 2-person bungalow. Also, we were past the age of 30, our careers were progressing nicely, and many of our acquaintances were having children. As I worked, I pictured the future, with the house finally finished, and was startled to realize that we would have huge amounts of time and energy to devote to something else in our lives. We had created the perfect setting for the addition of children.

This time I approached the decision from more than a philosophical angle. Already convinced that adoption was theoretically possible, I now considered the more practical and emotional aspects of the decision. Could we afford children? Could we care for children and continue our careers? What would children require from us? Did I really want to be a mother?

I decided that I did indeed want to be a mother. I thought we had plenty to offer kids, and I believed that we were creative and flexible enough to work out any financial and logistical problems. I wondered what Jim would think. We had not discussed children in a long time. I resolved to bring up the subject on my visit to see him in Oregon the next week.

* * * * *

My resolve about not adopting steadily weakened over the next three years. Slowly, my hardened heart began to perceive adoption as part of a solution, rather than part of the problem. There were a number of reasons for my gradual change in attitude.

Ever since our wedding in 1975, Darlene and I had anticipated raising a family. We really wanted to share our lives with children. We got along well with other people's children, and felt we could offer a loving, stimulating, and enriching home for our own. Like many others, we felt sorry for children who were abused or neglected, and wanted to help where we could.

On a less altruistic note, we were also afraid of growing old as a childless couple. Not that we wanted someone to care for us when we grew old, but we were afraid of turning old and suddenly regretting a decision not to adopt. We didn't want to miss out on all the wonderful experiences of raising children and sharing in their lives. We saw the joy our friends' children brought them, and we wanted some of that happiness for ourselves.

Darlene and I wanted more out of life than a house, a successful marriage, and satisfying careers. We wanted a family. For us, the Great American Dream became the desire for a child to join our lives. Finally, the question became "Where could we get one?"

We offered to take our best friends' daughter off their hands, but they wouldn't have it. We considered driving to Iowa and stealing my sister's kids, but quickly rejected that plan also. This left adoption agencies — public and private — which we contacted to check out our options.

At first, Darlene and I thought we wanted to adopt a baby. It seemed like the most natural thing to do. We soon learned, of course, that babies were in great demand, and the supply was correspondingly low. It seemed that nearly everyone who wanted to adopt desired a baby. The Department of Family and Children's Services politely informed us there was a 10-year waiting list to adopt a baby. Ten years seemed like an eternity to us, and lacking the patience of Job, Darlene and I simply couldn't wait that long.

In addition to our general impatience, there were more practical factors to consider, such as our own ages and general states of health. As it was, this would not be a case of a spry 18-year-old bringing up baby. I was already 32, so I likely would be 42 when we got the baby. This meant that I would be 52 when trying to play baseball with my 10-year-old. I already had back problems and wasn't at all sure that I would even be able to move two decades later. But the biggest stink of the whole thing was that there was no guarantee that after waiting a decade we would even get a baby. We decided to look elsewhere.

In talking to a number of private adoption agencies, we were happily assured of less wait. For the tidy sum of $25,000 (more or less — depending upon the agency), we were virtually guaranteed a baby in approximately 9 (!?!) months. No wonder there was a ten-year waiting list for the "free" county babies! The baby business had become big business. Anyway, without getting into a moral, ethical, or legal discussion on this, Darlene and I felt that the "expensive" babies would be adopted into "good" homes where they would be loved and well-cared for. So we considered further. What about all the children who were measuring their ages not in days or even months, but in *years*?

Unlike an infant, an older adoptive child comes complete with a past life which includes memories and experiences too numerous to count. Although it is possible to know much more about an older child than an infant, such as IQ, appearance, and physical abilities, the older child also arrives with an impressive list of "unknowns." The child is, after all, not merely the product of genetic engineering, but of past environment as well. All too often, that environment is found lacking in the basic qualities of life normally regarded as crucial for healthy physical, mental, and emotional development.

More than likely, the child has been removed from the birth parents because of their neglect or abuse and placed into foster care. Years may elapse while the parents struggle with their problems before finally relinquishing their parental rights in court.

By then, not only has the child's personality been formed, but basic attitudes and outlook on life have been shaped by previous events, many of which have been frightening, confusing, and painful. Already, at a tender young age, the child has established patterns of behavior (often self-destructive) for dealing with life as he or she knows and understands it. Having experienced physical and emotional neglect and/or abuse, the trauma of rejection, separation, and loss, and a life of insecurity, the older child is more likely to exhibit various types of acting-out behavior, such as lying, stealing, hitting, or running away. In social work jargon, the child is considered "hard to place."

Bad memories can fade and emotional wounds can heal, but it may take a very long time, and the scars remain. Lots of practice is required to learn new behaviors and develop trusting relationships. In the meantime, the child's past repeatedly gets in the way of both present and future, presenting numerous obstacles which must be overcome for a successful adoption and a happy home. Generally speaking, the older the child, the more severe the mental, emotional, and social problems have become and the more difficult they are to correct. Unfortunately, few would-be adoptive parents are willing to accept such a huge challenge.

It was while we were out West during the summer of

1986 that Darlene and I finally made the decision that would forever change our lives. I was working as a research technician for the Georgia Institute of Technology and was conducting an extended series of field measurements under some high-voltage power lines near Madras, Oregon. Darlene flew out for a visit. During a lull in the measurements, in the quiet solitude of the Cascades, we took a long look at our lives and decided to open our hearts to an older, hard-to-place child. Darlene contacted the Department of Family and Children's Services (DFACS) immediately upon her return to Atlanta. Placing our hopes and fears in the hands of God and our new DFACS social worker, Darlene and I waited for the future to unfold.

Chapter Two

Into the Great Unknown

While the hand of God had closed some doors in our lives, others were being opened, in the direction of becoming parents.

After a month-and-a-half long observing run near Madras, Oregon (during which time Darlene and I had reached our decision to adopt), I packed up the instruments and headed to Richland, Washington, for another four weeks of measurements. The day after I arrived, however, I was notified that the experiment had been abruptly canceled. I was not disappointed. Having been away from home for the past three months, I was really very anxious to get back. I quickly loaded up the van and returned to Atlanta.

The timing was perfect. Although there was considerable lab work to be done before our next observing run, I was able to take some time off to work on our house. I completed the plumbing, installed the furnace, and finished the basement. It was also during this narrow window of opportunity between research trips that Darlene and I were fortunate enough to be admitted to an adoption study group. We spent November and December attending weekly meetings with other prospective adoptive parents and several DFACS social workers.

The parents-to-be were, quite naturally, interested in children. The social workers were interested in *us*. Their mission, a difficult task indeed, was twofold. First, they were to educate us on the special problems encountered with adopting children. Second, and more fundamental, they were to ascertain our fitness for becoming parents. Before they were finished, they would scrutinize our thoughts, our feelings, our incomes, and our homes.

Our future lay in the hands of the social worker assigned to us. Although she was a wonderful woman and an excellent social worker, we nevertheless felt somewhat intimidated. Our future depended largely upon the evaluation of this one person. After our third meeting, Darlene wrote the following passage in her diary:

"Time creates new perspectives and dulls the urgency of any situation. We are in an adoption study group. I was very nervous about the first meeting, feeling like I needed to ascertain the competence of the social workers before I could feel comfortable. Now that I have approved them, I can get on with the business of them approving us."

Our adoption group ranged in age, backgrounds, and interests. Some of the people in our group had biological children; others did not. Like us, the other men and women were new to the world of adoption. We knew there was much to learn, and we soaked it up like sponges.

For ten weeks we discussed our marriages, our personality traits, our own family histories. We learned about child development, child psychology, and child discipline. We studied theories of loss, grief, and emotional re-attachment. We practiced problem-solving and conflict resolution skills. And we shared our hopes and fears about becoming parents. When children were introduced to our home, we would be ready!

With our diverse backgrounds — particularly Darlene's knowledge and skill as a social worker — we felt we could succeed in providing a home for older kids where other adoptive parents might waver. We knew that some types of behaviors and needs made adoption more difficult, and we believed we could handle some of these and provide a home for kids who might not find one otherwise. As we considered our options, we became committed to taking older, hard-to-place children.

As we attended the meetings, we felt more positive about adopting older children instead of babies. Idealistically, we believed school-age children would offer less immediate disruption to our lives. They would be able to participate in some of our recreational activities, such as traveling and camping. Babies, on the other hand, would — at least temporarily — cramp our lifestyle.

In addition, older children offered a certain measure of independence. They would be able to get dressed by themselves, communicate their thoughts, and attend school for part of the day. There would be no diapers to mess with, no car seat to install, and no stroller to push. They would be able to function without constant supervision.

However, we were not yet ready to deal with teenage issues. (We're still not ready, and those years are upon us.) So it seemed that four- to ten-year-olds would be perfect for us.

Unlike many adoptive parents, who adopt a single child at a time, Darlene and I decided to consider sibling groups. We suspected the family adjustment period would be traumatic for each additional child, so we might as well go through it with two or three at one time. We thought the kids might help each other if they were scared or angry. We also knew it was more difficult for agencies to place siblings together, and thought we could accept the challenges this might offer. In our minds, we had considered all the angles and were prepared for anything a small child or children could bring.

After the group meetings, our social worker made home visits. Did we have rooms for children? Had we considered school? We were asked to specify in more detail what kinds of children we thought we could handle (ages, behaviors, backgrounds). We got the water and septic tank inspected. We made a scrapbook with pictures of ourselves, our relatives, our house, and other information about us. This scrapbook would be given to our new children by their foster family to introduce them to us and to provide opportunities for them to talk about us during the transition to our home.

Our home study was completed in February, and we were approved by the state office shortly thereafter. Then, the long wait began.

Darlene and I had hoped that we would receive a child almost immediately. After this long approval process, we were ready for children. As the days grew into weeks, and the weeks stretched into months, we became more and more impatient and frustrated.

Much of our frustration stemmed from simply not knowing what to expect, and therefore not being able to make any plans. If Darlene had been pregnant, we would have had a fairly good idea of when to expect our children, and how many there would be. Because we were adopting, however, and had not specified any particular age, sex, or even number, we honestly had no idea of what we would get. We didn't know how to decorate their room(s). We didn't even know whether to buy building blocks or bicycles (or maybe some of each).

Meanwhile, I filled the time worrying about the duties and obligations of being a father. I was concerned that my present job as a research technician, though personally rewarding, was not exactly conducive to raising children. I was gone too often, for far too long.

But opportunity knocked, and another door opened. I learned that the laboratory where I worked was looking for a science writer in its communications department. With my technical and scientific background, my writing experience, and some superb lobbying on the part of my boss (to whom I shall forever be thankful), I landed the job. I would now be home nights and weekends, instead of taking field measurements in some distant state. I assumed my new responsibilities in May.

Later that month, Darlene and I finally finished our house construction, a four-year labor of love that would have tested the strength of Samson and tried the patience of Job. The effort we had put into building our house proved merely a precursor to the amount of energy we would expend in building relationships over the next six years. Our house was ready to bear the pitter-patter of little feet, and Darlene and I were as ready to become parents as we were ever going to be.

But still we waited.

As the year waned, we became somewhat resentful. Somewhere out there were children — *our* children — waiting for a home. And here we were, chafing at the bit to become parents. What possibly could be taking so long? We attempted to hurry things up a bit by calling our social worker regularly. She was sympathetic, but the wait dragged on.

Summer and autumn came and went. In November, Darlene was preparing for a two-week speaking engagement in England. The day before she left, our social worker called to inform us that we had been matched with *two* little boys: Christopher James (age 5) and Jonathan Gene (age 4). We excitedly arranged a time, three weeks distant, for a formal presentation of the boys' information to us.

Darlene was ecstatic. The long wait was over at last. Or was it? I wasn't sure. After all, we knew nothing of these children other than their names and ages. We knew nothing concerning their past, their problems, or their personalities. We didn't even know what they looked like. I was apprehensive. How could we be sure these were the right children for us?

Darlene shared none of my doubts or concerns. Upon returning from England, and against my good advice, she proceeded to tell the world that we were adopting two boys. Despite my desperate pleas, there was no stopping her. She wrote in her diary:

"I have been telling *everyone*, and have addressed announcement cards, etc., but Jim is still feeling like the announcement is premature before we are actually presented information about them. My sign of confirmation was the middle names. These children are meant for us, and we for them."

Granted, the boys' middle names had been quite an interesting coincidence. Chris' middle name was my first name. Jonathan's middle name was my dad's first name. While Darlene accepted this strange coincidence as a sign from God, I remained skeptical.

But, as I said, there simply was no stopping her. She even stood up from her assigned seat in the choir loft, and angelically proclaimed the news to the congregation of our small church, *before we had even met the children.* I shifted uncomfortably in my pew, tried hard to look happy and excited, then cast her a menacing glare. I was committed to this before I had a chance to decide!

Several days later we met with the DFACS social workers to learn about the boys (*our* boys, as Darlene so gaily put it). We were shown photos, and were told of the boys' family history. We asked lots of questions, to which we received lots of answers — some of which conflicted with one another. At the conclusion of our meeting, our social worker asked whether we wanted to proceed to the next step, which was actually meeting the boys, and required that we think about it at least overnight.

Darlene was all for it, of course. I was dubious. Among other things, we had learned that Jonathan had asthma. He was rather lethargic and couldn't breathe well much of the time. At age four, his prognosis was uncertain: he might outgrow it, or it might plague him — and limit his activities — for the rest of his life. His older brother Chris, at age five, had been diagnosed with a learning disability. He did not know his alphabet, could not count from one to ten, and could barely speak.

Although my heart was willing to accept these boys as my own, my mind reluctantly refused to cooperate. Darlene and I pursued a very active lifestyle. We enjoyed physical exercise, such as hiking, camping, gardening, and building houses. How could we continue this lifestyle if one member of the family couldn't participate? Also, knowledge and education were very important to us. Could we truly accept Chris with his disability?

After an evening of thoughtful discussion and deliberation, Darlene and I reached a compromise. We would ask for a "blind meeting," one in which we could watch the boys as they played, but they would be unaware of our presence. The agency understood, and readily agreed to our terms.

I realized that Jim was panicking now that the children loomed as a reality, a commitment that would permanently change our path through life. But I also realized that he really wanted to be a father, and like the experience of test-diving a new car, actually seeing them would melt any resistance standing in the way of his desire.

In theory, Darlene and I were to arrive at the DFACS office and watch the boys as they played in a special room fitted with a large, two-way mirror. We chose this for their protection as well as ours. We did not want to build the boys up for a potentially painful disappointment. If, after seeing the boys, Darlene and I were still interested in becoming their parents, then we would meet them, give them presents, and talk awhile. On the other hand, if we did not want to proceed, there would be no harm done. The boys would not have known about us. They had been to the office many times before and would believe this was simply another meeting with their social worker.

Of course, this isn't how it turned out. Apparently, someone had forgotten to tell the boys' social worker of our stipulations.

When Darlene and I dutifully arrived at our DFACS rendezvous on time, we learned that the boys were running late and had not yet arrived. We took a seat on a small couch opposite the receptionist's desk and waited patiently. We were confident that we would be called when the boys were situated in the playroom.

A few minutes passed. Then we heard the sound of a door opening, the shuffle of feet in the hallway beside us, and the muffled voices of two small children. I looked with alarm at Darlene, and she at me. Realizing what might happen, I stood up and searched in vain for a place to hide. But before I found a hiding place, a little head peeped around the corner, followed by the body of another child. The smaller boy glanced up at his older brother and asked, "Chris, are those our new mom and dad?"

I just stood there, dumbfounded, staring at the boys. This wasn't supposed to be happening — the boys weren't even supposed to know about us! Our anonymity had been lost!

After what seemed like hours of staring at each other, the social worker escorted the boys into the playroom, which, it turned out, was less than 15 feet from our sofa. Darlene and I quietly followed the boys into the room. *If only we had been a few minutes late*, I thought to myself.

We were formally introduced, and Darlene and I gave the boys the presents we had fortunately brought along *just in case*. The boys were as curious about us as we were about them. After we talked and played awhile, Chris read a book for us. Well, he tried to read a book, and his attempt was touching. Then we went for a soda and snack in the cafeteria. Venturing outside for a short walk, the boys ran around, and climbed a wall near a dumpster to show us how strong they were. (Before long, Darlene and I would be the ones climbing walls.)

Although the meeting had not gone quite as we had planned, we felt pretty positive about it. It was almost love at first sight. We decided these were the kids for us and arranged our next meeting.

Because of their ages, we had to move gradually through the transition into our home. After all, Chris and Jonathan were adopting us as much as we were adopting them. As our social worker so aptly put it, adoption is something you do with, not to, older children.

Our second meeting was lunch at McDonald's (with our first kids' meals, of course). A few days later, we picked the boys up from their foster home and took them to our house. They eagerly ran through the house identifying everything. They knew where all the rooms were from the scrapbook we had made months ago during our long wait. We ate lunch, played games, talked, and then it was time to return them.

Our fourth meeting, which was to be our first weekend spent together, did not start off very well. Jonathan's lungs were choked with phlegm, worse than usual. While Darlene and the foster mother were in the kitchen discussing what the boys liked, and did not like, to eat, Jonathan sort of coughed and threw up all over himself and me.

"Oh, great!" I sighed to myself, wiping sticky phlegm from first my hands, then my coat. "What have I gotten myself into?"

After a quick bath, Jonathan was again ready to go. His asthma continued to bother him all weekend. He just sort of sat around much of the time, content to be watching whatever was going on around him. Chris, on the other hand, had the energy of a puppy, though we understood only about half of what he did, and even less of what he said.

But both boys did their best to display good manners.

"See, we have good manners," they would say, as if trying to convince us that, if we adopted them, they would be perfect children.

A few days later, the boys came to stay with us for a week. During this time they became more comfortable with us, and we with them. It had seemed quiet and lonely without them. Yet it seemed so strange having little beings dependent upon us. As I watched them sleeping in their beds, the awesome responsibility struck me at last.

During the week, there were countless games where the boys would run off to a hiding place only to call out "come find me!" The boys' insecurity was showing. Did we really want them? Enough to go find them? Playing this game offered them early assurance.

Finally, the long-awaited day arrived at last: the boys moved in for keeps.

Jim and I transported the boys and all their worldly possessions in two cars amid a confusion of excitement and sadness. While Jim loaded the little tricycles and box of toys the foster family had given them for an "early Christmas," the boys tearfully said good-by and raced through the house one last time. Then, they and their two hamsters climbed into the back seat of my car and we headed home.

Seeking comfort from his hamster, Christopher opened its shoe box and let out a blood-curdling yell. As I screeched to a halt on the side of the highway and both boys burst into tears, I ascertained that the hamster had bitten Christopher, he had dropped the box, and the hamster had fallen under the car seat. Knowing the hamster to be an important connection with the foster family, I started frantically patting my way through bags of clothes, around boxes, and under car mats, (without opening the car doors, of course) in search of an escaped rodent that bites.

Finally lucky, I grabbed it, stuffed it back into its shoe box and comforted my children until we were calm enough to finish the trip home. We spent the rest of the day spreading out little treasures they had collected, putting together their new hamster cage, hanging up their clothes — trying to blend their familiar possessions into their new environment and helping them feel that their new home belonged to them.

We prepared for our first Christmas together, but money was tight. Very tight. There had been so many things to buy: beds, dressers, curtains, clothes, and toys (lots of toys). Darlene and I went without Christmas presents that year. But not the boys. We wanted this to be their best Christmas ever.

My former boss, who had two boys just a couple of years older than Chris and Jonathan, gave us a rocking horse, some toys, and three boxes of the nicest clothes you have ever seen. Some had never been worn, with price tag still attached, leading us to wonder if these were truly "outgrown." We gladly accepted.

Our families sent things as well. A financial gift from my folks went a long way towards meeting our financial obligations. Our church friends hosted a "kids' shower." Our first family Christmas was most memorable.

Chris and Jonathan had spent most of their lives with their foster parents. They had adjusted quite well to a foster care environment and were very comfortable calling their foster parents "mom" and "dad." Although they understood that Darlene and I were to become their new and permanent mom and dad, they could not refer to us by those titles at first. To them, we were simply "Jim" and "Darlene." Although we felt this was somewhat of an impediment to the necessary transition, on the urging of our social worker we let them call us by our first names.

It is rather awkward having your four-year-old son call you Jim. At home. At church. In stores. This went on for several weeks.

Finally, we felt it was time. We explained the situation to the boys. We no longer would respond to our first names. To get our attention, they had to call us Mom and Dad. They resisted. For a few days, it went like this:

"Darlene, can I have more juice?"

"What's my name?"

"Darlene, can I have more juice?"

"What's my name?"

"*Mom*, can I have more juice?"

"Yes."

They caught on quickly but began to display anger, refuse to follow directions, compare and reminisce about their foster family. The honeymoon period was over, and we were about the business of forming a family.

Chapter Three

Surviving the First Year

Like marriage, adoption is intended to be forever, for better or worse, for richer or poorer, in sickness and in health. Like a successful marriage, a successful adoption requires love, flexibility, and deep commitment. And like newlyweds, the newly adopted family experiences a brief honeymoon, a wonderful time when you basically enjoy just being together.

Enjoy it. I mean *really enjoy it*, because it won't last long. When the honeymoon ends, the adopted family enters a very trying period of readjustment.

At first our kids tried so hard to please. They did all the right things. They followed directions. They were kind, obedient, and courteous. They were "perfect" children. We, for our part, were patient and tolerant of their activities. We were fun playmates. We cooked all their favorite foods. We were "perfect" parents.

During the first couple of weeks, the kids were overloaded, with everything new and different. It was exciting. It was fun.

There were presents to be opened and myriad discoveries to be made.

Then one day it happened: the honeymoon was over. Without warning, our family suddenly found itself back in the real world. The novelty soon wore off, and the initial excitement gave way to anger, frustration, and disappointment, for both children and parents. The children's stress level had reached its limit. They could not handle any more new things. They could not handle the excitement any longer. Their emotional high had reached its peak, and they were over the edge.

Our children were adjusting to a new schedule and a new set of routines. They were going to bed, getting up, and eating at different times than they previously did. They were absorbing new surroundings, building relationships with new people, orienting to new rules, adjusting to a new culture. Their little bodies became physically exhausted and emotionally drained. Invariably, something broke down. They lost their thin veneer of control and began to act out with emotional outbursts.

The children began to recognize that what they had perceived as a vacation at the beginning was becoming a permanent change. (In our case, our insistence on being "Mom" and "Dad" signaled this change from temporary to permanent.) They now realized that they were having to give up their old way of life, and they did not like some of the changes at all.

What was neat, different, and exciting in the beginning became somewhat annoying to them, and to their parents as well. During the honeymoon, adoptive parents often ignore any number of things which could cause a confrontation. Things came up that we didn't like, but we overlooked it. We didn't complain about it. We didn't always correct it. We made allowances for it. We noticed it, making a mental note that our son would need some guidance in this area later, but we didn't say anything. Not yet.

Soon after Chris and Jonathan moved into our home, Darlene penned the following entry in her diary:

"The children are perfect. We have been surprised at how affectionate and cooperative they are. Of course, they both compete to be best and liked by us. Chris got mad at Jim, and later was overheard asking Jonathan if he was going to let Jim be his new daddy. They are so cute sometimes."

Well, *cute* is not the word I would have used to describe either Chris or his behavior at the time Darlene was writing in her diary. It was my first "run-in" with my oldest son, and I remember it vividly.

Who's in Control?

When I had come home from work that day, I had placed a roll of pennies on the top of my dresser. I intended to give each boy half of the pennies after dinner. However, when I later went to retrieve the roll, I noticed it was considerably shorter than it had been earlier. Someone had surreptitiously removed 18 pennies from the roll.

Both boys vehemently denied any knowledge of the missing pennies. Not until I found the missing pennies in one of Chris' drawers (carefully concealed in a sock) did he confess to having taken them. He said he had simply wanted them, so he took them. He appeared neither ashamed nor sorry.

Both boys were *very* curious to see what would happen next. Now, neither Darlene nor I wanted to make a big deal out of this, but we did need to communicate that stealing and lying were wrong and would not be permitted in our home.

We calmly explained that it wasn't right to take something that belonged to someone else. And, we briefly discussed the virtues of telling the truth.

I gave Jonathan his 25 pennies, told Chris he would have to wait a while for his, and stood him in the corner for a few minutes to think about the incident.

Boy, was he mad! Not because he had gotten caught, or even because he had been punished. No, Chris was angry because *he was not in charge.* The issue wasn't over coins, it was over control. Chris was rebelling against the new authority figures who had suddenly entered his life and been thrust upon him.

This little incident set the stage for many months of minor skirmishes and major battles, while we fought over who was in control. Chris pitted the stubborn will of a 45-pound, 5-year-old boy against that of a 150-pound, 33-year-old man. I now confess that at times I felt we were evenly matched.

Chris openly opposed us at every turn. When told to put his freshly laundered clothes away, for example, Chris would just stand there. With all the awful stubbornness a 5-year-old can muster, he would defiantly yell, "I don't want to."

Chris lost that first test case over the pennies. But he was not about to give up. The issue of control was still far from resolved in his mind. That's why, later that night while the boys were putting on their pajamas, Chris asked Jonathan if he was going *to let* me be his new daddy. The question of *who was really in charge* was very much alive and kicking in his brain, and he displayed his opposition to our parental role by rebelling at every opportunity.

I Don't Want To

Throughout our early months, Chris was angry all the time. Jonathan would leap all over us, but Chris would just stand there — very distant, very serious — always assessing the situation and carefully evaluating us. He showed no affection toward us, and resisted our attempts to show him love.

Chris' adjustment was extremely difficult. He was always comparing and questioning. He hadn't really wanted to leave his foster home. After a few weeks, he was ready to go back, and he clearly let us know it.

He constantly referred to his "other mom and dad."

"At their house we did this or that, went here or there, had this or that," he would say. Everything was bigger, better, and more beautiful at their home. I heard so much about life with his foster parents, I felt like *I* had lived with them.

Chris rapidly moved into the rebellion stage. When told to do something, like brush his teeth, feed the cat, or go to bed, he would just stand there and defiantly yell, "I don't want to!" Our patience began to wear thin.

One morning, Chris was in a particularly ugly mood. He refused to eat his breakfast. He refused to get dressed. And, he decided he wasn't going to school that day.

We let him skip his breakfast. If he didn't want to eat, fine. It wasn't worth a battle. But, he *was* going to get dressed, and he *was* going to school. We let him know, in no uncertain terms, what we expected of him. But it was to no avail. He firmly stood his ground.

As the minutes slowly ticked by, I grew increasingly impatient. I had an important meeting at work that morning, and really couldn't be late. When all normal attempts failed, I finally picked him up, carried him to his room, and dressed him myself. Then I carried him, kicking and screaming, out to the car. He was losing this fight, he knew it, and he didn't like it. A few minutes later he completely lost his self-control.

Here I was, driving 55 miles an hour down the interstate, in heavy traffic, and my kid was throwing a temper tantrum. He kicked madly at the floor, struck violently at the dashboard, and ripped at a small tear in the car's seat, all at the same time. He was an uncontrollable ball of fury.

I pulled off to the side of the highway. To catch his attention I reprimanded him across his rear. The action had little effect. By this time, the rip in the car seat had widened dramatically. The rear view mirror had been knocked askew. "This kid is destroying my car," I muttered to myself. Then I physically restrained him. His face turned scarlet, he sputtered, he screamed as loudly as he could, then he cried.

I held him until he finally got control of himself. Neither of us said a word. He glared at me the rest of the way to school. When I dropped him off, I slid over on the seat to kiss him good-by. He slammed the car door in my face. "We're in for a fight tonight," I thought glumly to myself.

Sure enough, that afternoon and evening he let us have it. In a marathon temper tantrum that lasted a full five hours, he hit the walls, kicked the floors, and screamed at the top of his lungs. He even threatened to kill us. He had actually planned how to do it while he was at school that day. He was going to stab us dead at night while we were asleep.

The temper tantrums continued almost on a daily basis as Chris worked out his anger and grief by hating us for our contribution to his life's miseries. Meanwhile, with Jonathan the issue of control took a totally different path.

At first, Jonathan couldn't seem to figure out anything. "I can't find my sock," he would state, standing at the top of the stairs. He wouldn't go look for it. He would just stand there and repeat "I can't find my sock" until someone found it for him. He was so cute that he usually got away with it at first, although we quickly realized that he was manipulating us.

When told to put his freshly laundered clothes away, for example, Jonathan would diligently attack the pile of clothes and put them away. He would hide them under his pillow, stuff them into his toy box, stick them back in the dirty clothes hamper. He would put them just about anywhere other than where they were supposed to go. No small wonder he could never find things when he needed them. Our boys' personalities were as different as night and day, but the issue was the same: *control*.

I'm Gonna Leave

I well remember the day that Jonathan announced he was leaving home. He had decided he no longer liked living with his mother and me, and he was moving out. He was only four.

"I'm just gonna leave," Jonathan muttered.

It was about the fourth time he had uttered those words in a single afternoon. The day had not been going particularly well and was rapidly progressing from bad to worse. Both boys had been naughty little buggers, testing the same limits over and over until both Darlene and I were virtually out of patience.

"Jonathan, go sit on your bed," I commanded.

"Well, I'm just gonna leave," he muttered defiantly for the fifth time, folding his arms and turning away from me.

"All right, go ahead and leave," I said. "I've had it. This is ridiculous. It's not worth it. Go ahead and leave. See if I care. Go on and go. Here, I'll help you pack your bags!"

Of course I said all this to myself. Part of me wanted to shout it out loud, because part of me felt it was true. But the better part of me bit my tongue. I slowly counted to 15 (counting merely to 10 doesn't always work), sufficiently calming down in the process. So, instead of blurting out those hateful, hurtful words, I gingerly stepped around his small form and dropped to my knees so our eyes would be at the same level.

"Jonathan, I don't want you to leave," I said. "I love you. You are my son, and I love you very much. It would make me very unhappy if you left." (I hope God forgives little white lies, I thought to myself.)

I can not say what thoughts, feelings, and emotions must have raced through his four-year-old mind at that critical time, but the transformation was quick and marvelous.

From that time forward, the words "I'm just gonna leave" were never again uttered from his lips. He really was begging for me to say "Stay! You don't have to like everything here, but you are loved anyway."

Imagine if I had actually told him to leave. Imagine if I had actually packed his bags. Where could he have gone? What could he have done? He would have been crushed, stripped of his dignity, his self-worth, and would have felt desperate, hopeless, and unloved.

I didn't say that he couldn't leave. Of course I never would have let him go. But by giving him the freedom to decide, he decided to stay.

Jonathan stayed, but the trauma of adjustment continued. After three months of emotional upheavals with our new sons, I was literally ready to give up. Darlene and I had been both happy and happily married for a dozen years. Now this.

Darlene wrote the following in her diary:

"The kids are ungrateful, whiny, mean, selfish, and dirty. My fear has passed, but my emotions need to catch up with my intellect. Here's where commitment counts. If I had any idea about sending the kids back, it would be easy to do. Acknowledging the feeling of wanting to, but not considering it as an acceptable option, is the only way for me to get through the tough days."

We thought we were doing something good. But at what price? Our altruistic naiveté was costing us dearly. My work life was suffering. Our home life was even worse. Darlene and I were fighting a good bit of the time about how to deal with the kids. Our sex life had died. We weren't sleeping together. In fact, we weren't sleeping at all. We were overburdened, emotionally drained, and preoccupied with all the problems. We looked, and acted, like zombies.

I had large, dark bags under my eyes, as did Darlene. I nicknamed her "owl." She called me "raccoon." We looked terrible, and felt even worse. We half-heartedly considered divorce, but neither of us was willing to take the children. I offered Darlene the house, the newer car, and generous alimony and child support, but no go. We simply had to make this work. At the ends of our ropes, we wondered aloud why we had ever gone through with this crazy, fool thing called adoption.

Our families lived several states away, so we looked to our friends for support. We received very little. Their responses, either voiced or implied, included:

- "You must be exaggerating...it couldn't possibly be that bad."
- "They're just *bad* kids. They would be doing this to anyone. It's not your fault."

- "It's all your fault — you must be rotten parents."
- "See, *I told you not to adopt.*"

Needless to say, such "support" was not helpful. Not having experienced adoption, our friends simply could not relate to what we were going through. What we needed most was an attentive ear and a sympathetic voice, not passing judgment upon us, but assuring us, instead, that what we were experiencing was a perfectly normal period of adjustment. A difficult time, yes, but one which, like everything else, would eventually pass into memory. We needed to hear that there was, indeed, light at the end of this long, lonely tunnel.

In desperation, we enrolled in a post-adoption support group. There we found the sympathy and empathy we needed. And, we were able to lend support to other traumatized adoptive parents in the group. We didn't pretend to have the solutions to their problems. And they didn't pretend to have the solutions to ours. But just sharing with others who were experiencing similar situations helped a great deal. We could openly express our anger, frustration, and disappointment, and be reassured that our feelings were normal, acceptable, and understandable. Sometimes, we even were able to really give or receive helpful suggestions about specific situations.

Saying Good-by

Because Chris and Jonathan had lived with their foster parents nearly their entire lives, they were deeply attached to them. To help them maintain this vital link to the past, in the face of a scary and uncertain future, we occasionally let them call their foster parents. We made sure they called only when things were going well at our house to prevent the foster parents from being an "out" for the kids during difficult times. If they needed or didn't like something, they had to deal with us.

Several months passed, but the boys were still mired in the past, unable to move forward. We arranged a visit with the foster parents at their house. There, the boys were relieved to learn that they had not been forgotten; that they were still loved by their foster parents, and always would be.

More important, the boys saw other children staying in their old room, sleeping in their beds. Because the foster parents had accepted new foster children, Chris and Jonathan saw that it was okay to get on with their lives: they were not being disloyal to their foster parents by loving us and joining our family.

That week, Chris had his last great temper tantrum, screaming for an hour about nobody wanting him and being unloved. He ended up crying himself to sleep. It was his way of letting go of his feelings of fear and grief and anger about his past and the beginning of his ability to connect with us as parents.

After the visit, both Chris and Jonathan made rapid progress in their attachment to us. Although we still talked about their life with their "other family," they did not ask to call or go there again. We had been a family now for eight months.

Chapter Four

History Repeats Itself

In the spring of 1990, little more than two years after Christopher and Jonathan had entered our lives, Darlene began hinting that maybe it would be a good idea if we adopted more children. At first I pretended not to hear. Then I simply refused to consider such a preposterous proposition. Weeks later, when push came to shove, I rather vehemently explained all my many reasons for thinking it was a dumb idea, the foremost of which was my memory of the first traumatic experience. Darlene dropped the subject, and I expected that to be the end of that.

Over the summer, our family frequently went camping, and one particularly fine weekend found us at Mound State Monument in Alabama. From out of the blue, Darlene again brought up the subject of enlarging our family.

"I'll discuss it later," I stalled. *Why ruin a perfectly fine family vacation?* I thought to myself.

That evening, after roasting hot dogs and marshmallows over a crackling campfire, we snuggled the boys into their sleeping bags and kissed them goodnight. As we sat together watching the deepening twilight, an owl hooted nearby.

"Now, about children..." Darlene began. She had not forgotten. One thing I should have learned about my wife by now is that she is persistent.

"Let's go for a walk," I quietly suggested.

As we slowly wandered around the park, Darlene presented all the pros (and I countered as usual with the cons) regarding adopting more children.

"Think of all the children out there who need homes," Darlene pleaded. "They need a father and a mother."

I had to admit that I rather liked being a father. My early fears had dissipated. I knew we were having a positive influence in the boys' lives, and they were doing the same in ours. Yes, it would indeed be nice to be able to do this for other children. My resolve was weakening, and Darlene sensed it.

"But, it was *so hard*," I protested. "Chris and Jonathan really put us through the wringer at first. Have you forgotten all the hassles and problems, all the *tantrums*?"

"It will be hard at the beginning, but we know how to handle the adjustment better now," she stubbornly insisted. "If we get kids about the same age as Chris and Jonathan, they will be older this time, so they'll better understand and be able to cope with what's going on. And having two brothers who've already been through adoption should help make it easier, too."

In the quiet solitude of the night, as we marched endlessly around the mounds, the negative arguments gave way to the positive ones, partly because we liked the idea of helping more kids, partly because we thought having a girl or two would be wonderful, and partly because we liked a challenge now and then. We decided to adopt again.

A few days later, we nonchalantly asked the boys how they would feel about having some more brothers and/or sisters. They took to the idea right away (although Chris half-jokingly asked if we could simply trade in Jonathan for a replacement). In fact, they rather liked the idea of having someone else to play with at home, in addition to each other.

But, they wanted more *brothers*, not *sisters*. Boys could play baseball, climb trees, and catch frogs, among other things. Girls...well, what would girls like to do? They conceded that girls might like to go camping or play with their stuffed animals. We explained that while we weren't sure what type of children we might get, their mom and I were thinking that a pair of girls might balance the family. Unconvinced that girls might actually be interested in basketball or riding bikes, the bright idea of siblings dimmed a little in their minds, but they agreed that we should pursue the subject further. A family decision had been made.

The following night at supper Darlene asked them if they had thought any more about the subject. Indeed, they had. Gender no longer an issue, both boys were now concerned about the ages of any new children coming into the family. Chris desperately wanted to remain the oldest; he perceived himself as the boss. Jonathan was equally concerned about *not* being the youngest. He admitted that he was tired of being told what to do by Chris, and didn't want to be directed by *everyone*. Darlene and I assured them that we would take their feelings into consideration, and that we would keep them up to date on what was happening.

Darlene contacted our former DFACS social worker, who was surprised and happy to hear from us. She was excited at the prospect of us adopting again.   She anticipated no problems with us being reapproved by the State through an update of our home study. Although we were veterans of the system, we were required to attend the training sessions again.   The content had changed slightly, and the State required attendance.   Anxious to make a good impression, we sat through a repeat of numerous sessions dedicated to behavior, discipline, feelings of loss, and the adoption process.   Although we did not benefit as much from the group this time, we were able to contribute our experience to other prospective adoptive families.

Darlene and I added another bedroom, large enough for two children.   We moved Christopher and Jonathan into it temporarily to help them anticipate some re-arranging of spaces.   We were now able to accommodate up to five children, depending on the gender combination.

We completed our home study in June of 1991, and were reapproved shortly thereafter. We dreaded the long wait that we feared was coming, not only for ourselves, but for the boys who wavered between excitement and disbelief that siblings were ever coming.

History repeated itself when the long-awaited call came in November. We had been matched with a nine-year-old girl and her seven-year-old brother. (This age combination happily met the requests of both Chris and Jonathan.) The children were not local, which presented certain obstacles, but the social worker wondered if we would be interested in learning more about them? We eagerly attended a meeting to learn about our new children (with Jim still muttering, "They're not ours. We don't know anything about them yet.")

Betty was a real extrovert. She liked everyone and wanted to be liked by everyone. Talkative and attractive, she tended towards dominating conversations, events, and situations. Betty would say and do just about anything to get attention. She was highly skilled at manipulating others, including adults.

Thomas was exactly opposite. Being an introvert, he turned his thoughts, feelings, and emotions inward; at times he absolutely refused to speak to anyone. Unlike his sister, Thomas had learned to protect himself from further hurt by rejecting all attempts at love and companionship. *"Who needs you?"* he would shout at anyone about to get too close. He was impulsive, quick to anger, and easy to frustrate.

Theirs had been a difficult past, one which included deprivation, abuse, and neglect. They had been in foster care for most of their lives and had moved for one reason or another almost every year of their existence. They had both had to wait a long time for their chance at a loving, permanent home.

Sadly, a recent attempt at an adoptive placement for them had resulted in a disruption. The failure of a permanent placement, for whatever reason, is one of the worst things that can happen to a hopeful foster child. It is another promise broken — this time perceived as a betrayal by the adoption agency or perhaps as a personal failure to ever measure up to anyone's idea of a good child. It opens painful wounds from past rejection and builds another layer between the need for love and the ability to accept it when offered.

As a result of their adoption disruption, Betty was even more outspoken and Thomas was much more withdrawn: both were more hurt and insecure than before. They wanted to be loved, but they would not be easy children to raise.

Sensitive over the previous placement attempt, the DFACS staff was naturally apprehensive concerning another placement. *The next attempt simply had to work out.* To help ensure success, the social workers were looking for prospective parents who had a successful adoption already under their belts. Somewhat awkwardly, Darlene and I had to somehow prove to the staff that we were sincere, could handle certain types of behaviors and problems, and possessed the commitment to see this new adoption through to a happy finalization.

To better prepare Betty and Thomas for their new placement (and partly to convince themselves that we were the right parents), the social workers suggested that we write a letter to the children. The letter was to accompany our family's life book, which would introduce us to the kids, and was to address a number of concerns:

• The social workers were apprehensive about the children moving to a totally different environment. Betty and Thomas had grown up in the country. Darlene and I, living in close proximity to Atlanta, were viewed as "city slickers." Our letter should help lay some of their fears to rest about this foreign place and lifestyle.

• The social workers wanted us to express our willingness to love and accept the kids as they were. In particular, the children were extremely sensitive about their first names which their previous adoptive parents had tried to change, against strong advice from DFACS workers. Quite understandably, the children had been confused by this. After all, they had very little in life except their names, and suddenly those had not even seemed good enough.

• The social workers wanted assurance that this adoption would be forever and some indication of how we would convince the children of this fact. This was especially important, since the children had been told all of this before, and it hadn't worked out.

On November 19, 1991, I wrote the following letter:

Dear Betty and Thomas,

Oh, what beautiful names! I bet you didn't know that my mother's name is Betty and that one of my very, very best friends when I grew up was named Thomas. Beautiful names for such beautiful children!

We are all looking forward to having you come live with us. We have been waiting a long time for you, and we want to be your "forever family" more than everything else in the world! We have prepared your rooms, and a very special place in our hearts for you. You are the very best Christmas presents we could ever get! We love you very much!

All our friends are waiting to meet you. The boys and girls at your new school are waiting to play games with you. Your new teachers and principal have promised to take good care of you and help you make new friends. The neighborhood children are excited, too. Even our cat, Puffy, is excited. She likes to get petted and brushed. Do you like cats?

We have a big house that we built ourselves and a big yard with lots to see and do. Sometimes we camp out in our back yard, and cook hot dogs and marshmallows over a fire. There are so many trees you can't even see the house. We also go camping in other places, and we like to fish, hike, hunt fossils, launch rockets, and make things.

And we like to share. As a family, we will share our love and learn from each other. What things can you teach me? I'm anxious to learn from you.

Thank you, God, for sending Betty and Thomas to us! We love you very much!

>Your New (and
>Forever) Father,
>*Dad*

The letter satisfied the social workers, and I'd like to think that it made a difference to the children. One day, more than two years later, I found Betty sitting alone, quietly pouring over its contents. She didn't say anything, and I didn't ask, but she cast me a loving smile.

On November 22, Darlene and I met with a combined team of social workers and supervisors from both counties. The children's histories were again presented to us, this time in much more graphic detail. It seemed as though the social workers were testing our reactions to each new fact — in essence, saying, "Hey, folks, can you handle this piece of news?...Okay, how about this one?" Darlene and I began to feel out-flanked and out-numbered. We had already committed totally to this adoption, and wanted to just get on with it. While we wanted to know all we could about the kids, once we had decided to adopt them, we weren't going to change our minds. We knew the social workers had the best interests of the children in mind, but then, so did we. As the day progressed, we grew weary of trying to convince them of this fact. We grew tired of all the scrutiny and wondered if we were passing the test. By the end of this day-long meeting 150 miles from home, Darlene and I were at last approved for this adoption. Finally clear of this major hurdle, we arranged to meet the children early the following week.

When we next arrived, I was in for a pleasant surprise. After all the social workers had said, I half expected to see horns sprouting from the children's heads. What I saw, instead, were two beautiful children who desperately wanted a family and a home.

We gave them each a small present, went out for a bite to eat, and then went for a walk. It was cold, and the kids nuzzled against us for added warmth. Here was potential for love, I thought. The kids were definitely not monsters.

Partly because of their ages, and partly because of the earlier disruption, the children's social workers insisted upon a gradual transition from the current foster home into ours. They didn't want the children overwhelmed, and neither did we. Consequently, over the next five weeks Darlene and I logged more than 2,700 miles shuttling back and forth for meetings and visits.

We were anxious for Betty and Thomas to see their new home and meet their new brothers. When the day finally arrived, the meeting proved a portent of things to come. Darlene had remained home with the boys, and I went to get Betty and Thomas. After a two-and-a-half hour drive, we at last pulled into our driveway. With the telltale sound of tires crunching on gravel, Chris and Jonathan rushed outside to meet their new sister and brother.

Betty nervously hopped out of the car. Thomas followed behind; slowly, hesitatingly, clearly uncertain about what would happen. I made the necessary introductions.

"Where's Fluffy?" Betty gaily asked.

"Her name is *Puffy*," Chris answered dryly. "She's over there." He pointed towards the patio, immediately unimpressed with his new sister.

Chris and Betty eyed one another carefully, each measuring up the other person. Their eyes assessed; their minds judged and evaluated. Chris was used to being king of his hill. Betty, similarly, had grown accustomed to being queen of hers. Very soon their respective hills would become one and the same, and the turf battles would begin. Betty finally sauntered over toward the patio in search of the cat.

"They'll get along just *great*," I remarked facetiously to Darlene, who had come out of the house to join us. She cast me a knowing glance.

"Where's the Nintendo?" Thomas asked quietly.

Jonathan's eyes lit up as he responded, "In the basement. Come, I'll show you." Jonathan and Thomas struck it off right from the start. They were both used to being the youngest. No sibling rivalry there....yet.

The children's visits gradually became longer over the next month. Frequent phone calls between visits assured them that we were thinking about them and looking forward to their moving in permanently. On December 30, they were finally allowed to stay forever.

Betty and Thomas' world had widened dramatically with their new placement. Despite all the background the social workers had shared with us, we were often at a loss to explain their behaviors or attitudes. We frequently misunderstood where the children were coming from and where they were headed.

On one of our family outings, for example, Darlene and I elected to drive through, rather than around, Atlanta. We thought Betty and Thomas would enjoy seeing the downtown sights. Their initial excitement was transformed into fear as we passed through the narrow corridors of steel and glass, mortar and concrete. The children cowered in the back seat. Somewhere nearby the sound of an ambulance pierced the air, and Betty tried to hide under her coat.

Neither child had been to a big city before, but they had watched television shows which portrayed highway accidents, police arrests, and all sorts of emergency situations. Unable to differientiate between the sights and sounds of crowds and traffic in real life and these television scenes, they were scared to death.

"There's so much we don't know about these children," Darlene admitted to me later that night. "They've brought so many memories with them. There's so much to learn about how we can help them grow up well." We were sure, however, that in many ways, history was repeating itself.

We again experienced the seemingly endless games of "come find me!" It seemed more awkward this time. Betty and Thomas were much larger than Jonathan and Christopher had been four years earlier, so they encountered considerable difficulty in finding effective hiding places. They were also older, perhaps too mature to be playing this game. In spite of their physical size, we knew that emotionally they were experiencing the same initial feelings of insecurity. Did Darlene and I *really* want them? Playing this simple hide-and-seek game offered them necessary assurance.

We also experienced repeat scenerios daily with such simple tasks as explaining family rules, bedwetting, introductions at a new school, teaching personal hygiene, and arranging for clothes, toys and other belongings for each child. With all these similarities, great differences also emerged between the first adoption and the second one.

Chapter Five

Temper, Temper

Unlike Chris and Jonathan, who had referred to us by our first names for well over a month, Betty and Thomas called us Mom and Dad right away. Perhaps they comprehended more because they were four years older, but it was surprising to us that they could use the words at all after having been bounced around from home to home so much. In fact, they used the terms Mom *and* Dad *so effortlessly, Jim and I wondered whether they really knew what the words meant. We know now that they clearly understood. Betty and Thomas wanted very much to have a permanent home, and using the terms Mom and Dad was their first major step at claiming that home.*

With Chris and Jonathan, our honeymoon period lasted a few weeks. With Betty and Thomas, there was no honeymoon. Sibling rivalry was largely to blame, as the children battled over position in the new family. Although Betty and Chris were the primary players, the competition between all four children steadily grew worse. Betty was taller, but Chris was older.

Jonathan was smallest, but Thomas was youngest. Chris was in a gifted class at school, but doing poorly. Betty was in a remedial reading class, but doing well. Thomas could play baseball best (Jonathan's favorite sport), but Jonathan was best at Nintendo, which was Thomas' favorite activity. Jonathan and Betty were in the same grade and argued over who had the best teacher and the hardest homework.

Jim and I struggled to help each child deal with feelings of inadequacy, anger, and jealousy. We tried to find opportunities for them to cooperate together. We had family talks about the uniqueness of each individual and the value of each person's contributions to the family. Nothing seemed to help much. Each day seemed to get off to a bad start as the children came to the dining room for breakfast.

They bickered constantly at the table, needling each other into fights. They fought over cereal, over milk, over bowls. They argued over who got the cereals first, who took the last of the favorite cereal, who had the most cereal, and who had to put the cereal away. The mornings set the tone for a bad attitude for the day. Finally, in a brilliant flash of genius, we enrolled them in the school breakfast program. They simply got dressed and left in the mornings, delaying any major opportunities for conflict until after school. While this didn't solve the problem, it did relieve the morning stress and we were able to make some progress on other agendas.

Older children do not enter an adoptive home with a clean slate. Often, the past they bring with them may include horrible experiences of rejection, neglect, and abuse. You can almost feel their pain.

The children also have a history of learned behaviors,

many of which are destructive and inappropriate in a stable, loving environment. They have seen, heard, and absorbed attitudes and actions which may seem disruptive, impulsive, senseless, violent, and shocking to the parents who have adopted them. After a month or so of getting acquainted, the novelty of these behaviors wears off, patience wears thin, and the reality of forming a permanent bond with these foreigners begins.

The children are also bound to experience some shock and disappointment with their new "forever families." No doubt, they have fantasized about what life will be like with their new parents. They have pictured in their minds the perfect house, neighborhood, school, and friends. They have their own ideas about how things are going to be. Suddenly, one day they realize things are *not* exactly how they had imagined. The big build-up becomes the big let-down, as realism sweeps away idealism.

Unfortunately, disappointment has been a way of life for these children. Now, as usual, there are again some things they don't like. Their initial excitement gives way to anger, fear, frustration, and disappointment. Their emotions erupt into all sorts of rebellious outbursts, as they attempt to return to familiar patterns. Changing these behaviors, which are caused by insecurity, low self-esteem, and past example, is not an easy thing to do. Living with the past can be extremely difficult.

Testing and Trusting

After a week in our home, Betty and Thomas were familiar enough with their surroundings, but they were unsure of what would happen in any given situation. Naturally, they began to test us to see whether we did things here the same way as their previous caregivers. We had experienced the testing phase with Christopher and Jonathan several years before, and were anticipating it with Betty and Thomas.

This second time around, however, proved to be much longer and had more serious consequences than our earlier experience. Our two new children were also testing to see whether or not they could trust us. Unlike Chris and Jonathan, they had learned not to trust adults. They had frequently been moved from caregiver to caregiver, and their earlier adoption disruption had proven a bitter disappointment that took a heavy toll on their ability to trust. They had heard all about "forever families" before. They had trusted, but in their experience families had turned out not to be forever. We had to earn their trust, and they tested us thoroughly.

A typical incident went as follows:

"Dad, may I ride my bike in the street?" Betty would ask.

"Yes, as long as you don't go past the mailbox," would come my reply. We live on a dead-end street, and I had explained several times that riding past the mailbox was dangerous because cars often do not stop at the corner.

A few minutes later, I would glance out the window and see Betty riding her bike well beyond the limit set by the mailbox, *and she was carefully watching the house to see if I had noticed.* I would immediately go out to the street.

"Betty, I said you could not ride past the mailbox. You disobeyed me. Now you must put your bike away for the rest of the day."

Without so much as a whimper, Betty would put her bicycle away and find something else to do. She seemed almost relieved to have been caught and disciplined.

Of course, it made perfect sense. Betty was testing me. If

I didn't mean what I had said about riding her bike past the mailbox, how could she believe me when I said things like "I love you" or "I'm going to be your dad forever"? To her young mind, a little punishment was well worth the added sense of security and trust.

This type of scenario was played out by both Betty and Thomas on nearly a daily basis for well over two years. It was imperative that Darlene and I be tough and consistent disciplinarians, both to build our relationship of trust and to curtail truly dangerous behaviors. To our friends and neighbors, we must have appeared to be unduly strict parents about relatively minor incidents. Our children's love and trust were highly dependent upon this strictness, and their ability to act without supervision would lag behind that of other children their age for several years. As they gradually learned to trust us, we could relax the supervision and grant them more freedom.

Early Rebellion

The honeymoon period with Thomas and Betty lasted only as long as the month of short get-acquainted visits to our house. Within days of moving in, they began rebelling against their new surroundings. They didn't like their bedtimes. (They used to stay up *much* later, they said.) They didn't want to do their homework. (They never *used to* have to do their homework. Why, they never even *had* homework before, they said.) They wanted to watch much more television than we would permit. (They *used to* watch any television shows they wanted for hours each day.) Thomas didn't want to go to school. (He *used to* throw a tantrum and would be allowed to return to bed in the morning.) Betty didn't want to take a bath or wash her hair. (She *used to* scream until she was sent to bed without a bath.) Some of their rebellion was trivial, some was serious, and some was downright comical, as with Thomas and his vegetables.

We have only a few rules at the dinner table. Each person takes whatever food they like from the combination offered. They must take one fruit or vegetable, and they must eat what is on their plate. Chris, Betty, and Jonathan were not finicky eaters; they would eat just about anything placed in front of them. Thomas, on the other hand, had taken an early disliking to fruits and vegetables. (According to him, he had never eaten anything even remotely resembling a fruit or vegetable.) We explained the virtues of fruits and vegetables, disguised what we could in the form of juice or dessert, and proceeded for a few days with only minor complaints.

One evening, Thomas helped himself to several large chunks of cooked broccoli. Why he had taken so much, I don't know. Broccoli was on his list of horrible vegetables. Throughout our meal, the green mass just sat there, growing colder and limper by the minute. When the rest of us had finished eating, Thomas remained at the table, two lumps of broccoli staring up at him. We told him he could get up from the table when he had cleared his plate.

He moaned. He groaned. A few minutes later he quietly announced he was finished, and took his now-empty plate to the kitchen.

"That was too easy," I thought suspiciously to myself. Upon investigating, I found his broccoli neatly hidden away in his napkin. I returned Thomas and his broccoli to the table and repeated the rule. Five minutes later he was again "through."

I intercepted him in the kitchen and suspiciously checked his napkin. There was no broccoli to be found.

Congratulating myself on a minor victory as I walked back through the dining room, I smiled. Then I stopped dead in my tracks. Scattered on the floor beneath the table were dozens of little bits of broken broccoli. About two large chunks worth, I estimated. I supervised Thomas as he cleaned up the floor, while Darlene got out two more pieces of broccoli for him. Thomas finally resigned himself to his fate and ate his broccoli. He even admits to liking it now.

"That really wasn't so bad," I thought to myself. This time I was right. Thomas' time of testing had not yet come. When it did arrive several months later, it came with all the suddenness and fury of a summer thunderstorm.

The Rage Stage

When Thomas came to us, he appeared shy and indifferent to much of what was going on. For example, when our social worker came by for one of her regular visits, timid Thomas remained in the background. Bouncing Betty, on the other hand, was all over the worker. She gaily showed off her room and belongings, chattering non-stop. Thomas didn't say a word. Finally, as the worker was preparing to leave, Darlene took the lead and encouraged her to see Thomas' room also. Thomas proudly showed off his room and belongings, but said barely ten words the whole time.

Other than Nintendo, Thomas displayed little interest in toys or games. He would play with other children, but he was a passive participant, and he would quit the moment someone did anything he didn't like. Throughout the early months in our home, Thomas coolly maintained an attitude somewhere between disinterest in anything in particular and anger at everything in general.

When troubled, Thomas would clam up and squirrel away in his room. He absolutely refused to tell us what the problem was, and no amount of prodding could loosen his locked lips. Thomas silently withdrew to a quiet corner in his mind.

Chris was the first member of the family to make the unfortunate discovery that, when angry, Thomas would hit rather than talk. The kids were playing baseball one afternoon, when Thomas slugged Chris for tagging him out at first base. Chris was shocked. Repeated episodes over the next few weeks resulted in a new house rule: anyone hitting another person could not play with others for 24 hours. This didn't totally solve the problem. Thomas continued to hit, and we soon learned that he would hold a grudge and eventually get even.

One day, Jonathan was dismayed to find one of his favorite possessions — a toy he had brought with him from his foster home — broken into bits, its pieces lying scattered throughout the house. Thomas had gotten quite angry with Jonathan earlier that week and had looked for an opportunity for revenge. Thomas did finally apologize, but he didn't stop getting even, and he still refused to discuss his feelings.

A few months later, Thomas suddenly surprised all of us when he unexpectedly flew into a rage stage. Almost a year after he had joined our family, he finally began to express himself verbally. Now, when he got mad, which turned out to be fairly often, he would run up to his room and scream bloody murder — literally. He was going to kill *Mom*; he was going to kill *Dad*; he was going to kill *Jonathan*. He never threatened to kill Chris or Betty, perhaps because they were bigger and not as forgiving as Jonathan. Thomas had lurched from extreme silence into overwhelming verbal tirades.

Fortunately, the bulk of this phase passed quickly. Thomas' emotional pendulum finally equalized as he mastered the fine art of expressing himself less expressively. Thomas slowly learned to talk through his problems and to punch his pillow instead of people.

The Terrible Tantrums

Thomas' silence stage had been frustrating, but not too difficult for the family as a whole. Betty became our immediate problem and concern. Her acts of early rebellion rapidly grew into a more serious situation. She seemed unhappy with us, with herself, and with life in general, and she managed to dump all of this discomfort on the rest of us. She was extremely critical of other family members, and wholly uncooperative much of the time. Betty was also very manipulative. She frequently used this skill simply to stir up trouble, mostly in attempts to receive attention, as the family tried to resolve whatever situation she had caused. For example, there was the time about the timer.

Christopher, Betty, and Jonathan were all studying piano and practiced 15 minutes each day. They kept track of the time with a small kitchen timer.

On this particular day, Chris practiced first. When his time was up, he dutifully went upstairs to inform Jonathan it was time for *his* turn. Jonathan went downstairs to practice, but promptly returned to report that the timer was broken. I went downstairs to investigate. The front dial to the timer was missing.

"It was fine when I used it!" Chris protested.

I split the children up in pairs to search for the missing dial. The Chris/Thomas combo finally located the missing part — in the piano bench.

It was time for a family powwow. I explained that the dial had not fallen off, opened the piano bench, jumped in, then closed the bench all by itself. Someone had helped it.

Much to my chagrin, *no one confessed.* In fact, all four children vehemently denied any knowledge of the incident.

Suddenly, what was initially a very small thing grew to larger proportions. Someone was lying. I did not know who had hidden the dial, but I had my suspicions. Trying to give the culprit an opportunity to apologize, I announced that I expected the guilty party to confess within one hour's time.

An hour later Chris sought me out.

"Has Betty confessed yet?" he asked.

"Well, no, as a matter-of-fact she hasn't," I replied. "And what do you know of the matter?"

Chris explained that after telling Jonathan it was his turn to practice, he had gone to the playroom for a toy and had seen Betty take the timer apart and hide the dial in the piano bench (that's how he knew to look there during the search). Betty had not noticed him at all. I asked him why he had not told me sooner.

"Because I thought it was important that Betty confess," he told me flatly. "You know, she lies a lot."

I confronted my daughter. I told her I knew she had hidden the dial, and that it was important that she admit it.

Betty denied everything. She conjured up an unconvincing story of how Chris had really done it, just to get her in trouble. I again stated the importance of telling the truth, and I gave her some additional incentive to admit her mistake by informing her she would be grounded one day for every five minutes that elapsed until she apologized. I fully expected her to confess immediately.

Boy was I wrong! Hours passed. We ate dinner in relative silence. Finally, just before bedtime, Chris politely informed Betty that she was now grounded through the end of March, which was nearly one and a half months away!

Betty let out a wail, then screamed, "Fine, I did it, okay?" She ran off to her bedroom where she sobbed herself to sleep. We enforced the punishment for two days, and then granted her parole.

While writing this chapter, I asked Betty about this incident. She remembered it quite clearly. She admitted that she was mad at Jonathan for some reason, and was just trying to make him mad. Well, she had actually succeeded in making us all mad.

Betty's actions aimed at others soon took a significant turn for the worse, and she frequently had the whole household in an uproar. The smallest things would set her off into screaming temper tantrums. If she didn't want to do her homework, take a bath, or go to bed, a major battle ensued. When bored with this tactic, she looked for ways to irritate her siblings.

At first, we tried the standard fare of disciplinary tactics. We tried offering her alternative ways of expressing her feelings. We discussed rules and the logical consequences for breaking those rules. We tried time-out; we tried standing her in a corner; we tried sending her to her room; we tried withholding privileges. Nothing seemed to work.

Betty's actions brought back memories of Chris screaming, "I don't want to!" at the top of his lungs. Betty, however, was older and bigger, and she would lash out at anything in her path. She possessed the physical size to add credibility to her words.

You can physically control a five-year-old. A nine-year-old is another matter entirely. When placed in a chair for time-out, she would simply get up. When placed in a corner, she would not stay. When escorted to her room, she would leave just as soon as you did. Her acts of open defiance dared you to take further action.

Betty would scream and yell. She would shout threats. She hurled insults along with shoes, books, and almost anything she could reach. Betty destroyed her toys, games, and her clothes. In an attempt to keep her from hurting herself, and to protect others from the frequently launched missiles, Darlene and I removed *everything* from her room except her bed. When she was out of control, we placed her in her room and locked the door, forcing her to remain there until she calmed down. All of this may sound like child abuse, but what the Kloeppel family was experiencing was more like parent abuse. In our attempts to discipline our daughter, we were hit, bit, kicked, scratched, spit at, and slobbered on. The emotional abrasion continued almost daily for months.

Betty's behavior was extremely stressful to other family members. At one point, Chris finally broke down. With tears streaming down his cheeks, he cried, "Why did we do this?" He wanted things back to the way they were prior to Betty and Thomas. I didn't tell him at the time, but so did I.

Both Thomas and Betty required nearly constant supervision and problem solving on the part of their new parents. Each new situation presented more obstacles to overcome. We spent untold hours discussing our approach to child-rearing, our methods of discipline, our seeming lack of progress with our newest children. We tried our best to be loving, understanding, and sympathetic, but it was difficult at times. In addition to fulfilling the role of parents, we often had to function as detective, judge, and jury for the multitude of incidents now occurring in our home. Meanwhile, we were also trying to meet the needs of our other children, whose behavior was deteriorating in response to what they saw happening on a daily basis.

Patience Perseveres

Betty's uncontrollable tantrum phase lasted a solid six months; Thomas' had lasted only half as long. However, both children continued to display defiance and destructive behavior intermittently for the *next year and a half*, and would return to these behaviors when tired or when experiencing any significant changes in their schedules or activities for several years.

In reality, our children's anger had little to do with our family. This was the most loving and secure home they had ever experienced. We knew it and so did they. Why, then, did they act this way?

Thomas and Betty in particular, were angry about their past. They were mad at their birthmother for giving them up for adoption. And they were mad about spending most of their lives in foster homes. They were mad that life was not going the way they wanted it to, and mad because they really didn't know how to make it any better. All this repressed anger and frustration had finally come bubbling to the surface and controlled their very beings.

In addition, both Betty and Thomas were extremely insecure. They were afraid that this adoption, like their previous placement, would not last. As a result, they felt vulnerable. Despite our constant assurance that we were their "forever parents," the children were afraid to commit to this relationship for fear of being hurt once again. Could they *really* trust their future to us? Would we *really* still love them if they acted badly? They were determined to find out and they continued to test this over and over for months and months.

Sibling rivalry also complicated our second adoption. In addition to new parent-child relationships, all four children had to work out new relationships with each other, and figure out their spots in the sibling hierarchy. Perhaps Darlene and I inadvertently made this task harder by adopting children who were all approximately the same age.

The problems we encountered this second time around were bigger because our children were bigger. They took longer to solve because our children were older. Betty and Thomas were physcially harder to manage, they were more likely to hold a grudge, and they had more practice with destructive behaviors. We could not expect to repair all the damage of a lifetime in one short year.

For the first year, we muddled through. Our previous adoption experience gave us courage and hope that the testing and tantrums stage would eventually pass, but at times we wondered if the first adoption had really prepared us at all for this second attempt.

As the year passed, we became convinced that part of our difficulty in forming a family emotionally was a result of the slowness of the agency process to legalize the adoption. While we continued to have major behavior problems with the kids, the agency was reluctant to finalize the adoption. They were concerned that the adoption wouldn't work out. We felt that we would continue to have major behavior problems as long as the kids knew the adoption wasn't final. They continued to display signs of insecurity, testing to see if we would give them back to the agency.

Up until the very day we went to court to finalize their adoption, Betty claimed she was not going to go through with it. She threatened to tell the judge that she hated us, that we hated her, that we mistreated her, and that the only reason we wanted to adopt her was because we wanted her to do work around the house.

We hired a lawyer and went to court anyway. The proceedings were, as anticipated, very cut and dried.

Finally, the judge asked if anyone wanted to say anything.

Jonathan just sat there motionless, his mind seemingly a million light years away. Thomas was stone silent, as usual. Chris looked totally disgusted, but knew better than say anything.

Then Betty boldly raised her hand. Darlene looked at me, and I at her. We both shifted uncomfortably in our seats, and stared uneasily at our daughter.

"Yes?" inquired the judge.

Betty cleared her throat. "I just want to say that I think it is a good idea that Jim and Darlene adopt us. (This was the *only* time that Betty had ever used our first names.) I think we should join the family....I just wanted to say that."

I just about fell out of my chair, but couldn't help wiping a tear from my eye. Our daughter was finally coming around.

Chapter Six

For Their Own Good

I remember very little of my life before my sixth birthday; Darlene is fortunate that she can remember further back. Where there are gaps in our memories, the voids are easily filled by the recollections of our parents, amply supported with thick family scrapbooks and photo albums.

Not so with adopted children. Because our children have been removed from their birth parents, they cannot augment their earliest memories. There are few surviving photographs, and even fewer pieces of "hard copy" such as birthday cards, report cards, or awards. In essence, our children have been stripped of part of their past; and these voids may never be filled.

In addition, our children have been unable to sort out or share some of the memories they do retain. They may repress pieces of the past associated with intense fear or pain, they may not have the vocabulary yet to describe what they have experienced nor the ability to put the memory in context of other events, and it may take a very long time for them to feel safe enough — and loved enough — to bring up embarrassing or hurtful memories from the past.

Our children were raised by others for a good part of their childhood. There's no changing that. Unfortunately, the daily events that helped shape their attitudes, beliefs, and behaviors are largely unknown to us. Their past is very much like a puzzle, with all too many of the pieces missing.

Bringing older children into our home was very much like turning on the television in the middle of a program. Since we missed the beginning, we initially had no idea of what was going on in the story. Television shows, however, are easy to figure out: real life is seldom so simple. Not having witnessed their earlier life experiences and having no history of their reactions and motivations to draw upon, for awhile we simply had no clue of what was really happening with them. While not knowing can be anticipated during the first few months of an adoption, it can have an unsettling effect when it surfaces unexpectedly months or years into the adoption. There was the time, for example, when our youngest son, Thomas, struck out of baseball.

Three Strikes and You're Out

Thomas had played on a baseball team one summer while in one of his foster homes. He told us how much he had enjoyed playing, and proudly displayed a photograph of himself, handsomely decked out in full uniform, on the front of a baseball card. He reveled in his brothers' envy that he had done one thing that they had not. Soon all three boys were begging to play on a team. Finally, two years later, they got their chance.

Before we signed them up to play, we held a family powwow at the park. In order to practice with the team three or four nights each week, we explained, the boys had to keep up their grades in school and continue to handle their daily chores without a fuss. Otherwise, they would be off the team. The boys readily agreed to our terms.

Almost from the time we signed the boys up, Thomas began acting out. He refused to do his homework; he refused to help around the house; he began intentionally to wet the bed in defiance when he was reprimanded; and he was rude to others most of the time. Darlene and I reminded him of our agreement and warned him that if his behavior did not improve, he would not be allowed to play baseball. We thought he was testing to see how far he could push the limits. Not wanting him to miss baseball, we re-explained consequences and gave him several chances to improve. He only acted worse.

For over a month his behavior steadily deteriorated. Thomas never made it to the first practice. He continued to act up at home (strike one); he had to be removed from the Wednesday night kids' activities at church (strike two); and he began to create disturbances at school (strike three). Darlene and I finally had to pull the plug. Thomas was out of baseball.

We expected the tantrum of the century. Instead, Thomas threw his baseball shoes away in one brief fit of anger and very quickly returned to normal. We were amazed and confused, but in the ensuing weeks were able to figure out what had happened.

Acting out was Thomas' way of controlling a snowballing situation. In reality, he had not wanted to play baseball at all.

Contrary to his bragging, his previous baseball experience had not been particularly wonderful! Some of the other children had ridiculed him when he struck out and had told him that he didn't play well. He was afraid this might happen again. After all the big talk to his new brothers for two years, however, he could not admit to his fear nor easily say that he didn't want to play on the team. Thomas was caught between a rock and a hard place. He knew that by intentionally misbehaving, Darlene and I would pull him off the team, so the solution was neatly in his hand. As we placed this puzzle piece into the proper hole in Thomas' life story, we wondered again if we were ever going to figure out enough of the unknowns to help our kids grow up.

The Need to "No"

Early on, we tried to give our children praise and positive reinforcement whenever we could. Acceptable behavior was rewarded with compliments, special treats and privileges, hugs and kisses, happy-face stickers, etc. However, we soon learned, as do all parents, that we could not always simply ignore unacceptable behavior. Discipline sometimes involves providing motivation to extinguish negative behaviors, and not surprisingly in our case, we found that the older the child was at adoption, the more behaviors there were that needed work.

All children need plenty of attention, and our adopted children often were so starved for attention that we found it impossible to fill their needs. Both in an attempt to gain more attention and in anger that their needs had not been met, our children began to exhibit temper tantrums, show off, irritate others, and frequently disobey. The negative attention that they received became better than not enough attention. In addition, the lifestyles which they had witnessed often included violence, lying, vulgar language and actions, and impulsiveness — not good examples of how to deal with life's frustrations.

Picking the best method of disciplining them was, at best, a shot in the dark. Words alone were seldom sufficient to change their actions. Often, we found we had to support what we said with a more substantial consequence. Whatever form that took — from "time out" (where the child sat by himself for a few minutes) to grounding (where specific privileges were forfeited for a longer period of time) — we learned that the consequence must be immediate and certain, and it must be enforced firmly and consistently. Initially, we had no clear idea of what had — and what had not — worked with these kids in the past. In fact, the children's past sometimes became a very big obstacle to disciplining them in the present.

Frequently, adopted children have been assured of consequences that have not been consistently enforced, have received punishments seemingly unrelated to their actions, have been promised rewards that never materialized, and/or have lived in several different environments with different systems of discipline. Our second two children had experienced all of these situations, and it took a very long time for them to make the connection between behavior and consequences on a regular basis. In our family, they also tried to push us into scenarios with which they were familiar — trying to force us to behave like others in their past had acted — rather than adjust to our way of doing things.

For example, Betty and Thomas had learned not to take

what adults said seriously unless the adult yelled, swore, or hit them. It seemed much easier at times to yell at them than to calmly repeat directions over and over with no discernible results. Our children were more comfortable and felt more in control with chaos.

It was maddeningly frustrating to be a consistent disciplinarian at times for children who were all pushing for different results. They seldom learned from each other's mistakes. They each needed to build a library of experiences to offset earlier years. Each pushed the envelope to see what lay beyond.

For example, one fine morning our daughter Betty went into a roaring temper tantrum and adamantly refused to get dressed. Darlene took her to the office in her pajamas (the three boys went to day camp). Betty was suitably embarrassed. She never forgot the experience, never refused to get dressed again, and never mentioned it again...until Thomas similarly acted up about a year later.

It was a Sunday morning, and Thomas simply refused to get dressed for church. After three warnings, he still sat on his bed in stony silence. When the time to leave arrived, he unhappily went to church in his pajamas.

Betty had seen it coming but hadn't said a word. For once she was totally on the sidelines, watching and waiting. She was extremely curious to see if the same rules that had applied to her were to be equally enforced with her brother. On the way home from church, Betty reminded Thomas that she once had to spend a *whole day* at mom's office in her pajamas, but that she had learned her lesson, and he would learn his, too.

Thomas, like Betty before him, learned a great deal from this little episode. He learned that when his parents say it is time to get dressed for church, they mean it. He learned, once again, that family rules apply just as much to him as to the other children. And, he learned to trust his parents just a little bit more. If Mom and Dad mean what they say about getting dressed, then they mean it when they say they love me. It was a difficult lesson, but one certainly worth learning.

If at first you don't succeed...

Major life changes can be stimulating, exciting, and rewarding. They can also be scary and confusing. Almost always, they bring numerous adjustments and higher — albeit temporary — levels of stress.

In the summer of 1993, Darlene graduated from college, culminating four years of very hard work and adding two masters degrees to her already impressive list of college diplomas. With graduation came a new job in a new career, and a new lifestyle for all of us. I took advantage of our new-found financial freedom to leave my full-time job and pursue a free-lance writing career. For our children, the next few months brought new schedules, new routines, and new opportunities to push the limits.

Amidst all the change, the children went to pieces. They became uncooperative, argumentative, and disobedient. They bickered constantly. They talked back. They couldn't get through a day without fighting among themselves or with us. In an attempt to solve the problem, we tried to supervise their every moment. Routine household tasks took all evening to accomplish. Homework was forgotten or lost. Structuring their time didn't help. They "just didn't feel like" taking a bath or picking up their belongings. Soon, we weren't raising a family at all, we were running a boot camp! And matters only got worse. We couldn't seem to get a handle on anything that helped.

Our patience again wore thin. It seemed that each day, one of our children was having a "bad day." We teased that they were drawing straws to see whose turn it was to be difficult for their parents. The levity did little to lessen the gravity of a worsening situation. Soon, it seemed as though our entire family life had become focused on discipline problems, negative attitudes, and destructive behaviors. We knew that major changes could trigger fears or memories of previous life changes, but had no idea it could be this severe.

At first, we calmly explained and discussed. Or tried to. It was like talking to dead people. Next, we tried several reward-punishment tactics, but these didn't work well, either. Eventually, we got angry and yelled and lectured a lot. The kids felt bad (so did Jim and I), but they didn't act any better. It seemed they were bent on destroying any semblance of family that we had. Weeks turned into months, and we got very tired. Finally, in an attempt to break the cycle and restore some household peace, we simply got tough. Jim and I took a look at how we had been contributing to the cycle by arguing about how to handle various situations, and agreed on an approach. We rearranged our daily schedule to disrupt any habits that were regular problems, and we developed a plan.

We sat the children on the living room couch. After an initial explanation of the "new plan," along with a review of procedures to accomplish all the expected tasks, a brief time to answer any questions, and an assurance of our determination to make our home a more constructive environment, we began. We did not allow any playtime until a daily written list of homework and chores was completed and checked by a parent. They were given only one opportunity to do homework assignments each day. Problems with completing the chores resulted in more chores — no discussion. We simply isolated — without discussion — any child demonstrating an uncooperative attitude to either us or to siblings by removing them to their bedroom for the rest of the day. Bedtime was advanced by one-half hour to reduce the amount of time available for problems to occur and to give us more time to wind down from the day. Attention of any kind was removed until the daily tasks were accomplished without incident.

Of course, each child had to thoroughly test the new system, and we still occasionally lost our tempers, but in general the plan worked well. Before too long, our children began to demonstrate cooperation and problem-solving behaviors. As they did, their playtime returned, they were allowed to be around other people, and we didn't yell as much. Yes, we still have an occasional "bad day" —with six of us it's hard not to — but we began making steady progress again and concentrated on developing the more positive aspects of our family life instead of battling constantly over the most basic daily activities.

Two Steps Forward: Three Steps Backward

Chris was five when we adopted him. We knew he was delayed in his speech development and began to help him by talking to him as much as possible, playing letter and word games, and reading to him every day. He seemed to make progress in this area, but went backwards in others. He began to suck his thumb and wet the bed frequently, although he was adamant about being a big boy, not a baby.

Adopted children, like other children, often regress to earlier stages of development when experiencing stressful situations. They also sometimes need to make up for stages in their lives when development was interrupted by a foster placement, trauma, or other circumstance. Quite by accident, I discovered a way to help Chris experience being a baby (and safely taken care of) without his objection.

Chris and I were the early risers in our household, and often I would sit to watch the sun rise above the trees in our wooded yard. Chris wanted to share this time alone with me in the quiet house and, since the chair where I sat was only big enough for one, I would hold him on my lap. We would talk, and I would cuddle him under the guise of not letting him fall off (he did not like hugs any other time). As soon as someone else got up, he would leave my lap and find something else to do. We did this for about a year before he lost interest. Toward the end of this time, he was able to stop sucking his thumb, with a little encouragement, and the bed-wetting became a rare occurrence.

Thomas, too, seemed to require a trip back into his skipped childhood years and couldn't progress any farther until he had experienced it. Thomas had grown older and bigger, but not more emotionally mature. In many ways, he was like a toddler. The world scared him. While seemingly tough on the outside, he often made it clear that he did not want to grow up.

When he became comfortable enough with us, Thomas plunged back into his earlier childhood, ready to claim what should have rightfully been his. For a while, he needed us to make even the simplest decisions for him, including what to wear and what to play. He reverted to baby talk. He wet the bed. He sat on our laps. Now, I am not a large man, and quite frankly, it was a little awkward having my 8-year-old son, who was nearly as big as I am, sitting on my lap and cuddling like a baby. But, it *was* necessary, and it didn't last *too* long. Thomas was finally able to move on.

Success At Last

In the fall of fifth grade, Betty asked if she could join a girls' basketball team that was being organized at a nearby park. Darlene and I discussed our concerns with one another before agreeing to sign her up.

We had two problems with Betty which occurred on nearly a daily basis. One was doing her homework. If she wasn't "in the mood," she could drag out a simple, 15-minute assignment all night, and make us all miserable in the process.

The other hassle was bath time. Betty could spend an hour fooling around in the bathtub and still not get clean — especially her hair. Nor would she dry her hair. This particular problem had persisted for years, through several foster homes. In fact, her last foster mother had grown so tired of battling Betty over this issue, she simply chopped off her hair (a rather harsh form of logical consequence). Betty wanted her hair to be long. We wanted it to be clean.

We had agreed to try baton lessons at her request earlier

in the year, on the condition that these two behaviors improve. Betty, still unable to connect her behavior with rational consequences and still constantly testing to see if we meant what we said, refused either to do her homework or take a bath in order to gain extracurricular privileges. She didn't make it to the first practice.

We agreed to try again with basketball, hopeful that this time the activity would motivate her. We discussed Betty's behavior with her, and laid down a few ground rules for the basketball season. She would not be permitted to go to practice or to a game until her homework was satisfactorily completed. And, since she would have to bathe after each practice or game — which generally extended past her bedtime — she would be allowed only 30 minutes in which to take her bath and wash and dry her hair. She again agreed to our terms and we waited to see if she had learned anything from her previous lesson.

Practices went well. Betty was a little late for the first few, on account of not completing her homework promptly (she just *had* to test us). But, she did not miss a single practice, nor was she late for any of her games. After practice, Betty dutifully took her bath, washed her hair, and dried it completely. She managed to uphold her end of the bargain very nicely. This was a major turning point for our daughter, and incidentally, for giving 100% of her effort during practices and games, Betty received her team's "Most Valuable Player" award. It was a good season.

Chapter Seven

The Haunting Past

After we adopted Chris and Jonathan, people who met us for the first time assumed that the boys had been born to us. (Interestingly, because of their young ages, they also assumed Darlene and I were much younger than we really were.) Occasionally, the subject of adoption would arise, and our new friends would be genuinely surprised to learn that the boys were adopted.

This all changed when Betty and Thomas joined the family. Suddenly, we had four children so close in age that it was biologically impossible for all of them to be our birth children, and the two most physically dissimilar children were in the same grade at school. Even a cursory introduction seemed to require some kind of explanation about our family composition as the topic of our children's ages inevitably arose. The children were often present at these introductions, listening to what we would share. We decided to respond honestly and briefly to the inevitable questions — they're all adopted; they came in pairs; we got them from the state adoption system; their birth parents were unable to take care of them. After that, we changed the subject.

Of course, some people were curious about our adoptions, and some were interested in the adoption process itself. We discovered quickly that there is a big difference between curiosity and downright nosiness. Amazingly, questions that normally would be discussed only with close family or friends seemed to become fair game for near strangers, almost as though the adopted child's past should be paraded (with as many lurid details as possible) for the entertainment of the listener.

While we tried to be open about our kids' adoption, we felt uncomfortable discussing much of their past lives with others in casual conversation. Once information was known by others, we had no control over how it would be perceived, acted upon, or relayed back to our children. We did not want people gossiping about our kids or making inappropriate comments to them.

We did make a special effort to give appropriate information to certain individuals as needed. We found that telling teachers about our children's adoption during the first few years helped the teachers to plan better lessons. For example, when Chris was in kindergarten, his class made Mother's Day cards. Chris, having been recently adopted, was in a dilemma over which mother (birth, foster, or adopted) should get the card. After a brief conference with his teacher, Chris ended up making more than one card. The teacher, using her increased awareness, explored different types of families with the students and discovered that almost her entire class lived in either single-parent families or step-families.

New acquaintances, however, were not the only people

who were curious about our children. For some time after our first two boys were adopted, we deliberately avoided certain areas of town to prevent constantly dredging up memories and encountering people from their past who were curious about their new home. After awhile, when an occasional errand took us near these areas, enough time had passed that we could talk as a family about the memories they sparked without emotional fallout for days afterward. But even Atlanta, with over two million people spread over 200 square miles, wasn't big enough to prevent chance meetings.

The first time a stranger approached us, Christopher and Jonathan had been with us for almost a year. We were in the check-out line at the grocery store. A woman walked up to the boys, gaily asked them how they were doing, bubbled about how much they'd grown, and demanded to know their new last name.

I quickly intervened.

"Yes, Chris and Jonathan have been adopted," I said. "I'm their new mother. The boys are doing fine."

I was cordial, but refrained from giving her any specific information. My mind was racing! Who was this woman? How should I respond?

Undaunted, the woman informed me that she was a friend of the boys' former foster mother and wanted to report how the kids were doing to her. She inquired about what school they attended and where we lived. Shaking inside, I again answered vaguely that the boys had grown up, and that we needed to pay for our groceries. We returned to our car and just sat.

Neither boy had the slightest idea who this woman was.

We talked about the incident together briefly and then dropped the subject. Both boys promptly forgot the scene, but for the next few days, I rehearsed in my mind possible responses to strange people who someday might approach us in stores. A few weeks later, Jim had his turn.

An Uncomfortable Surprise

A few months after adopting the boys, I went to lunch with Jerry, one of my best friends from work. We went to our favorite Mexican restaurant, where they served us tantalizing platters of tacos, enchiladas, and refried beans. Jerry is twenty years my senior, and takes meals in a slow, deliberate fashion. You don't rush Jerry when he is at the table. We were about halfway through our meal and on only our second bowl of chips and salsa (the chips and salsa were free — all you could eat), when in walked my sons' foster father.

I nearly choked on my taco. *What if he recognized me!* Supposedly, the foster parents did not know where we lived or worked — in order to protect the children. This was way too close for comfort.

I grabbed Jerry by the arm and exclaimed, "We've got to go...*now!*"

Jerry looked at me in surprise, then in disbelief. Then he looked longingly at his plate for a moment or two. He glanced back at my face and could see my fear.

Wordlessly, he got up from his half-eaten meal. We hastily paid for our food and slipped silently from the restaurant. We quickly climbed into my car and headed back to the office.

Part way there he finally asked me, "Okay, what gives? You in trouble with the law or something?"

Having gathered my wits, I explained the situation.

Jerry understood. And, bless his heart, he didn't pass judgment. He agreed it was an awkward situation, but I never knew whether he felt the conditions had fully warranted an interrupted meal.

What was most important to me was that at the time, Jerry hadn't questioned, he had only acted. As a friend, he owed me that. And as a friend, I owed him something, too. Over his protests, I bought him lunch the next day.

In retrospect, I now admit that I probably over-reacted in fleeing the restaurant. But in all honesty, I must also admit that I would probably react in much the same way if it happened again today. Although we have discussed the adoption of our children openly, having my children's past pop up unexpectedly in an otherwise routine day is still rather unnerving.

For the Record

Chris was halfway through kindergarten and already behind academically. He couldn't learn the alphabet, couldn't speak correctly, and couldn't sing any songs. His early learning difficulties were attributed to a lack of early childhood attention and adoption adjustment. Chris spent the next year and a half catching up. He took speech lessons at school, he played with educational toys at home. We tutored, we took field trips, we made sure he got enough sleep and ate his vitamins. At the end of first grade, Chris' tests qualified him for the Talented and Gifted Class, and we breathed a sigh of relief and pride.

For the next three years, however, we became increasingly

frustrated as Chris' performance in school declined. His teachers called conferences to discuss his uneven work — some assignments were superior, while others were sloppy and incomplete. His tests showed that he had the ability, so motivation must be the problem. We tried various disciplinary techniques in our attempt to motivate him. None, however, worked very well or for very long. In our search for suggestions, we again were amazed at others' comments.

"Oh, he's adopted," they would say, as though that explained any fault he might have. "We can't expect much from him," they warned, "since he might have had terrible experiences. He might never live up to his potential." We should have known that adopted children would present impossible difficulties, they implied.

Chris still could not recite the entire alphabet after passing third grade, although he had an above average vocabulary and was a fair reader. We became convinced that Chris had specific learning problems. We began to identify tasks that he could or could not do and to keep track of the assignments that Chris was not finishing.

Chris liked giving presentations; he was a good artist; he had creative ideas; he understood concepts; he could sit still; he had good social skills. Chris was easily distracted from concentration; he could not remember more than two items in a list of directions; he had trouble with spelling; he could not sound out words in reading; he could not remember the words to a simple song; he didn't complete assignments which required much writing.

I remembered that we had been told when we adopted Chris that he might have a learning disability, since he had speech development problems. I began to read about teaching techniques and learning disabilities. I monitored his diet to check for allergies causing chemical imbalances. One day, I gave him some simple tests that I found in a book on sight and hearing disabilities and became convinced that he had an auditory processing problem. The school psychologist tested him. The school audiologist tested him. No hearing difficulties surfaced, but Chris could not repeat sequences of numbers for the hearing test. We met again with teachers and staff to discuss test results and explore options.

All of Chris' school records were brought for review to this meeting. As we thumbed through pages of teacher notes and reports cards, Jim and I were shocked to see Chris' birth name on all the records from his first kindergarten. We had been assured that the name would be changed when the record was transferred. These records would follow our children wherever they attended school. At our request, the principal later substituted our last name in all the appropriate places.

Also buried deep in the file were evaluations, done when Chris had entered kindergarten, indicating the potential for a learning disability and listing the specific learning tasks with which he might have problems. The list was virtually identical to the one we had accumulated. He had an auditory processing and short-term memory dysfunction, which a small dose of daily medication improved dramatically. But by now, he also had several bad study habits and a reputation for inconsistent work, which he had to overcome. Yes, Chris was adopted, and there is some evidence that children who are adopted at older ages experience more problems with memory disorders. Adoption did not prevent Chris' progress, however, as much as misconceptions about adoption did. Again, looking through the school records, we realized how much about our children's short past we didn't know.

A Blast from the Past

The call came on Mother's Day. Darlene's mother was visiting us from out of state. Darlene was still at school. I answered the phone while hastily preparing dinner and conversing with my mother-in-law.

"Can I speak to Chris?" asked a feminine voice on the line. I called Chris to the phone.

I remember thinking that the voice didn't sound like that of a youngster. Nor did I recognize the voice as belonging to one of Chris' friends. But I was in a hurry, and assuming it was one of his leaders from our church, I handed him the phone.

I wasn't paying much attention to Chris' conversation, but since the phone was in the kitchen where I was cooking, I couldn't help hearing him ask, "Who is this?"

My ears perked up. I was curious about who was calling my son, as the kids weren't using the phone much yet.

"*Who?*" my son asked again, puzzled.

The conversation continued, and I lapsed again into preparing dinner and chatting with my mother-in-law.

Listening out of the corner of my ear, I heard Chris say in a low voice, "No, I don't think that would be a good idea." He hung up the phone, but remained seated at the counter.

I cast him a sideways glance from the stove and nonchalantly asked who had called.

"She said she was Linda's sister," he quietly replied.

"*What?!*" I half gasped, half demanded, nearly dropping my spatula.

"She said she was Linda's sister," he repeated, looking at me in a strangely serious manner.

My mouth fell open. I was dumbfounded. I cast my

mother-in-law a wary glance. "Linda is Chris' birth mom," I managed to murmur.

Forget about dinner. I walked over to the counter and, trying to hide any alarm in my voice, slowly asked Chris, "What did she say?"

"She said she was Linda's sister, and she asked me if I wanted her telephone number. I told her no, I did not think that would be a good idea."

Warning bells clanged in my head. How had she found us? Where did she get our telephone number? What did she want? Was it really Linda's sister? Did Linda even have a sister?

Thoughts raced frantically through my mind. Perhaps it was one of Chris' (or my) friends playing a practical joke, albeit it in extremely poor taste. But no, the caller had used Chris' birth mom's name, and neither Darlene nor I had ever told that name to anyone (and we still haven't, Linda is *not* her real name). I doubted if the boys had either. It was one of our to-be-kept-in-the-family "secrets."

Darlene's mother quietly slipped out of the room so I could be alone with my son. Bless her heart, she knew this was serious. She, Darlene, and I would have a long talk later that evening.

I tried to imagine what Chris was thinking and feeling at the time, but I'm afraid I came up rather empty handed. This was more up Darlene's alley, and I wished she would get home soon. I took a rather pragmatic approach, telling Chris that I didn't know if it was Linda's sister who called, that I didn't know if Linda even had a sister, but I would find out. I told him not to worry about it; that everything would be okay. And I told him not to tell his brothers or sister about the call until we knew for sure. None of this was particularly reassuring, but it was the best I could manage at the time.

When Darlene arrived home, I quickly took her aside and told her what had happened. She was as shocked as I had been. She suspected the call was legitimate: either it *was* Linda's sister, or it was Linda herself. Darlene agreed to call our adoption agency (DFACS) social worker the following day to report the incident, and to discuss possible strategies for dealing with this situation. We agreed not to tell the other children until we knew more, and we decided not to let the kids answer the phone for awhile.

Darlene was very concerned about Chris. How did he feel about the call and the possibility that his birthmother had suddenly reappeared in his life? Was he afraid? Was he excited? Why had he declined the offer of his birthmother's telephone number? For us? For him? Would he regret this decision later? In either case, we didn't think it was fair to put a 10-year-old child in the position of having to decide, and we were angry that she had done so. She should have identified herself and gone through us, the adopted parents.

I sought out my oldest son and found a private place to talk. He reviewed the phone conversation and his under-standing of what had happened. We speculated about possible reasons his birthmother might be looking for him and Jonathan right now. Chris was stunned by the call, curious about what his birthmother wanted and a little worried that he would have to make a choice between mothers. I tried to assure him that, while I also had questions about her and was upset about how she had contacted him, we were interested in his feelings and he would not be leaving our family. He intuitively knew it "was not a good idea" to get her phone number or meet her without involving us and was relieved that we would follow up in finding out what she wanted.

The next morning, Darlene dropped her mom off at the airport and called our social worker. We needed to know if Linda had a sister. We needed to know how she had found us. And, we needed to know what to do.

The social worker was amazed and alarmed by our story, and she was at a loss to explain or understand how it could have happened. She assured Darlene that she would check the agency's files, consult her supervisors, and get back to us with any information as soon as possible.

When I arrived home from work that afternoon, the kids had already arrived home from school and were waiting for me on the front porch. There was a message waiting for me on the answering machine from our social worker requesting me to call back right away. Something in her voice compelled me to do so immediately.

I got her on the first ring.

"Jim, I wanted to let you know that we received a call from Christopher and Jonathan's foster mother today. She said Linda does have your name, phone number, and address. The birthmother has visited the foster mother several times in an attempt to get information and has reported that she has driven past your house several times. We don't know what she is likely to do, but we think you should go to the police station and explain your situation. You might want to consider taking out a restraining order to keep her away."

I didn't wait to hear more. I said that I would go do it now and talk to her later.

I quickly called the kids into the front room and told them

that Chris and Jonathan's birthmother had been looking for them and had found out where we lived. We weren't sure what she wanted, but that our social worker had suggested I go to the police station and ask them what we should do. Then I packed them into the van and drove to the local police station.

The desk sergeant was kind but offered little help, or even encouragement for that matter. I was referred to someone in another office, who referred me to the clerk of the court, who refused to let me see the judge and sent me back to the desk sergeant. Growing frustrated and irritated, I finally realized I was on a wild-goose chase. I decided to go home and get better instructions. On the way home, I had to stop for gas.

When we finally got home, I told the kids I had to make another phone call, and instructed them to start on their homework. But before I reached the phone, there was a brief skirmish in another room. I responded to Thomas' crying. While they were getting their school books out, Jonathan had hit him...hard.

I promptly escorted Jonathan into the living room and was about to lecture and punish him when I suddenly caught myself. This behavior was totally unlike Jonathan, who was normally a kind, loving brother. I noticed he seemed very agitated, on the verge of tears.

I took him in my arms on the sofa and, momentarily setting aside my own problems and concerns, asked him what was wrong. I really should have known already.

Swiftly, the story spilled out of his shaking little body. Sobbing, he told me the trip to the police station had frightened him. While I had been arguing with the clerk of the court, some prisoners in handcuffs had been marched past the children in the hallway. And, when we were at the gas station on our way home, he thought he had seen his birth-mother in the next car. He was afraid she was coming to take him. He was, quite understandably, scared to death.

In my haste, in my over-zealousness to get a handle on the situation and protect my family, I had not truly considered the impact upon my children. I held onto Jonathan and comforted him until he calmed down. He apologized to Thomas, and I called a family powwow.

I told the children I was sorry for frightening them. I explained that I had simply over reacted. I reassured them that nobody was going to come "steal" them. Inside, I wondered if it was true. So they would feel better prepared and have a chance to talk about their concerns, Darlene and I talked with them again later to discuss possible actions if the birthmother did show up unexpectedly.

I called the foster mother directly as soon as the kids were in bed. She was expecting my call.

No, she hadn't given the birthmother any information about us, although Linda had been calling and stopping by the foster home at unannounced intervals for the past four years. She kept wanting to know where the boys were and if she could have pictures. This was merely annoying to the foster family, and they had not seen the need to concern us. However, now that the birthmother had obtained our name and address (through illegal means, she said), the foster mother had grown alarmed and had notified DFACS at approximately the same time that we had called them. She, too, was concerned about how the birthmother had obtained this information, as they were also adopting a child.

The birthmother called our house repeatedly. She was trying to reach one of the boys, but only Darlene or I would answer the phone. Many times we picked up the phone only to have it click in our ear. Dozens of calls registered on the answering machine...but no messages. Darlene and I began to feel nervous every time the phone rang. We were living on the edge and grew more apprehensive by the day.

The kids felt it, too. Jonathan began standing in front of the window, silently watching our driveway and the street beyond. Thomas started wetting the bed again. Betty wondered whether her birth mom was also looking for her. If she was, would she find her? If she wasn't, *why not?* Chris fantasized that the "other home" might have less rules to follow or would treat him with special privileges, and then felt guilty and disloyal for having these thoughts.

On Jonathan's birthday, at 9:30 at night, I answered the phone.

"Can I speak to Jonathan?" queried a female voice.

"No, he is in bed. Who is this?"

Expecting another "click," I was surprised when the voice answered, "This is his mother...."

The birthmother had finally realized that she could not get to the kids without identifying herself. She explained that she thought often of them, wondered if they remembered her, and wanted pictures.

I was unsure. "She wants more than pictures," I thought. "She could have gone through the adoption agency to request pictures." I asked how she had found the boys.

She responded that she had hired a detective and had used some "illegal avenues" but wouldn't give details.

I let her know that we recognized her needs and assured her that the boys had not forgotten her. I also conveyed that we did not appreciate her approaching Chris without our knowledge and were wary of her intentions.

She got angry and stated that all she wanted was to see them.

"How do we handle this?" I wondered to myself. "This is her request, not the boys'. We need time to plan what to do. Maybe if we see each other face-to-face, we can work out what she needs and what we need."

We made no promises, but offered to meet with her the next day at a restaurant in downtown Atlanta.

Neither Darlene nor I slept well that night. Imagined scenarios of the forthcoming meeting played through our heads. Over and over, we rehearsed possible conversations, trying to prepare ourselves for what might happen, anticipating what she might want and how we could respond. We had always considered the possibility that our children might want to find their birth families at some point, so we weren't particularly threatened by this meeting. The timing was earlier than we had anticipated, however. We were hesitant to establish an active relationship while the children were young and wanted to avoid conflicts about parenting them. We were actually relieved that the clicking phone would stop and we could finally address some issues with her, although we were concerned that our confidentiality had been breached and that her approach to us so far had not been a constructive one. We knew the children were ours legally, and we were confident of their love, but we were concerned for their mental and emotional well-being.

Our social worker offered to attend the meeting with us, but I politely declined. Darlene and I had to do this by ourselves. We didn't want to greatly outnumber the birthmother and thought we had a better chance of finding out her intentions if we were alone.

The agency supervisor thought it would be a good idea if I took a camera along to snap a photo of the birthmother. If the kids knew what she looked like now, they wouldn't be afraid of everyone they saw. I accepted the idea, but for an entirely different reason...I wanted to take a photo so I could give it to the police, if necessary. Darlene didn't want to take a picture at all at this first meeting, feeling that it would indicate a desire for a personal relationship before we had decided best how to respond. We finally compromised on taking the camera, but not using it unless we both agreed.

In our anticipation, Jim and I arrived at the designated meeting place early. We waited. The appointed time came and went. Still we waited. We paced around for an hour longer, inside and outside, but the birthmother didn't come. In all our possible scenarios, we had not even considered the possibility that she wouldn't come. We felt disappointed and confused. Then, a long-forgotten comment made years ago by the kids' social worker flashed through my mind. The birthmother had often not shown up for scheduled visits with the kids when they were in foster care, leaving them disappointed and wondering what had happened. She was doing it again...and my anger flared! My sympathy for her needs vanished, as my desire to protect my children from hurt grew to irrational proportions.

We decided we wanted DFACS to intervene on our behalf. We were still willing to meet with Linda, but we were not willing to play any games nor involve the children without a meeting first. She could call DFACS to arrange a meeting.

The agency sent her former social worker to her home to see what she needed, offered to arrange a meeting, and met with little success.

The birthmother called us later that night. I told her we were sorry she had not come to the meeting and that she should arrange a meeting through DFACS if she wanted to talk with us. We would not continue to take her phone calls at home. The conversation ranged from tears of regret to threats of taking the boys away from us, until finally I hung up.

We had another family powwow that night. We explained to the children all that had occurred and stressed that we would go on with our activities as usual. We acknowledged that we might see or hear from their birthmother in the future, but we had prepared them for that and would not let it bother our lives right now. We could still talk about it whenever they wanted. We prepared the school and day camp personnel for the possibility of her appearance, and tried to resume our normal routine.

For the next few weeks, the answering machine was full of no-message calls as we refused to answer the phone. Darlene picked up the phone early one morning, expecting a return long-distance call. A repeat of the previous conversation with the birthmother occurred, and again Darlene hung up.

Linda called back later that day and left a message on our answering machine which said the kids were better off with us, that we were the parents now, and that she wouldn't bother us any more. When I had finished jotting down her message on the notepad next to the answering machine, I penned two words of my own: "We'll see." As it turned out, that time she finally did quit calling. She has never tried to arrange another meeting with us.

We think the birthmother got what she really wanted — she made sure that her children hadn't forgotten her. In our case, they had not anyway, and we think the cost to our family to reassure her of this was far too great to justify her intrusion into our lives at this time and in the manner she chose.

Darlene and I still wonder how Linda found us. She said that she obtained the information illegally. But there are other paths possible, as we found out. Georgia is a closed adoption state. By law, an adoption agency's files — which contain relevant family histories, medical records, and other personal information including birth names and addresses — are to be kept strictly confidential. When an adoption is finalized in court by a judge, the respective file is "sealed" by the agency and no longer accessible. In addition, the original birth certificate is replaced with a new birth certificate which registers the child under the adoptive parents' names, and new social security numbers are assigned. In theory, this protects not only the child, but the birth parents and adoptive parents as well.

Unfortunately, the present system does not go far enough in safeguarding the identities of all parties concerned. In reality, sealed does not always mean confidentially locked, and a paper trail may exist which can identify adoptive families.

Our family lives with the uncomfortable knowledge that since Linda knows who we are and where we live, she could call or show up unannounced at any time. Even if we were to move, the problem would remain. She has our name; she could find us again. While I may have been indifferent before, now I am a firm advocate of locking records. Families of older adopted children have enough challenges to face, enough problems to solve, and enough obstacles to overcome without the added confusion offered by the intrusion of a birth parent who does not consider the child's needs. The child can face these issues later in life with more maturity and ability to cope.

Yes, I felt Linda's pain. And I'm sorry I couldn't do much about it. A piece of my heart truly went out to her. But, a far bigger chunk went out to my children. Their interests and needs had to come first. Adopted children — like all children — have a need to grow up in a loving, secure family environment. They should not have to stare out windows or glance over their shoulders in order to feel safe.

Chapter Eight

Living and Learning

What do adoptive parents need more than anything else? *An occasional night out.* Darlene and I recognized our need for a night out long before we acted on it. In fact, two months elapsed after Chris and Jonathan moved in before Darlene and I ventured out the door alone.

All parents need to get away for an evening, to take time off to enjoy each other's company unburdened by the responsibilities of parenthood. This is especially true when adjusting to an older child with unceasing demands. For us, the process of actually leaving proved more complicated than finding a babysitter, however. When we mentioned going out for an evening, the boys became agitated, and we became concerned about how they would react to our absence.

We felt Chris and Jonathan would feel more comfortable if they were left with someone they had seen before, and we realized that we needed to prepare the boys for occasions when we would be gone for any length of time. We hired a young woman from our church to babysit for an hour one Saturday afternoon. As the time of our date approached, the boys grew nervous about us leaving. We assured them that we would only be gone a little while, and *that we would come back*. But they had heard those words from others before, and it hadn't always been true.

For our first date, Darlene and I simply went for a short walk around our neighborhood. When we returned home, the boys tried to hide their relief at seeing us again.

A few weeks later, Darlene and I went out to dinner at a nearby restaurant. We hired the same sitter, and called home often. We arrived back home well before the boys' bedtime, so they could see that we had returned. This gradual transition to an entire evening out helped the boys feel more secure, but for a long time Chris, in particular, disliked us going anywhere without him.

One time, for example, Chris was very angry with us for leaving him and Jonathan at home with a babysitter. During our absence, he threw a baseball against a wall in my office, dimpling it nicely. The babysitter was apologetic, Chris was defiant, and Darlene and I were both concerned about Chris and irritated about the wall. I had recently painted that room, and had used up every last drop of paint. I did not relish the thought of repainting the *whole* room again. Darlene suggested a wonderful alternative: why not hang a bulletin board over the hole? We did just that, and I learned to *always* keep some paint in reserve for potential repairs.

Although we did not get out as often as we would have liked, we did get out far more often, in fact, than when Betty and Thomas joined our family. Unfortunately, we found few babysitters willing to take on four children at one time, and fewer still ready to tackle the types of problems our children were then presenting. Other than a long weekend when a dear friend offered to give us a much needed break, nearly six months passed before we were comfortable enough to step out for even an evening. And that night, while Darlene and I were gliding gracefully across a dance floor, pandemonium was breaking loose at our house.

Jonathan and Thomas had decided they were tired of being bossed around by everyone and were going to leave. After being sent to bed, they simply walked downstairs and out the front door in their pajamas, carrying flashlights and stuffed tigers. In all fairness, they really couldn't have gone far, not having anywhere to go. Upon realizing the boys' disappearance, however, our panic-stricken baby-sitter rushed to her car and pursued the fleeing boys down the street. She quickly collected them, then tried to collect her wits.

Feeling fully justified in their indignation and encouraged by the commotion they had caused, the boys plotted an escape from their second-story bedroom window. When they broke the window trying to remove the screen, however, they soon convinced themselves that the distance to the ground was too great for safe exit and abandoned that plan in the hope of a not-too-severe punishment when Mom and Dad returned.

This time, it was the babysitter who had had enough. Many more months passed before Darlene and I could again go out to dinner or see a movie by ourselves. While this babysitter did agree to come again occasionally, it was on the condition that we allow her boyfriend to accompany her and help her handle the children.

Our constant search for babysitters often meant that Darlene and I did not go out as frequently as we would have liked. We thought it would have been nice to live closer to our families for support during these times, and we will forever be indebted to a few of our friends who came through for us in a pinch. But, despite our occasional need to get away alone, our main focus remained connecting with our new children.

Forming a Bond

I put my tiny son over my lap, head down, and thumped him on the back until he choked. We were bonding.

When Jonathan first arrived, he seemed a little lost. In unfamiliar surroundings, he reacted to the absence of his foster mother by seeking a replacement caregiver. Beginning what seemed to be a random search, he would attach himself to any female adult who happened to appear friendly. While he consciously called me "Mom", he was emotionally adrift, grieving and confused in his new environment.

We had to watch Jonathan carefully in stores and at the park. One minute he would be next to me, and when I turned around, he would be wandering away behind a woman who had smiled at him as she passed us in the aisle. Sometimes, when he became really overloaded, I watched his eyes glaze over and become vacant for a few seconds. I wondered if he might be having mild epileptic seizures, until I realized that he was just shutting himself down long enough for his brain to catch up with his panic.

During the long winter months, I learned to give percussive treatments to clear Jonathan's congested lungs. This task was necessary whenever a cold combined with his asthma, making his breathing difficult. I believe that it was during these times, when I held him and pounded the phlegm out of his lungs, that he began to turn to me with trust.

Unlike Chris, who at first refused physical affection, Jonathan became an extension of my body. If I sat, he sat on my lap; if I walked, he held my hand. He liked to be picked up, cuddled, and kissed. He began to count on me when he was in pain and to seek comfort in my touch, and I gradually became Mom to him in feelings as well as in words.

Hut, Two, Three, Four

Thomas and Betty were too large for lap-sitting when they arrived at our house, but both were desperate for physical attention. They would compete for the front seat next to me in the car, grab my hand before another sibling thought of it, or demand a hug frequently during the day just to be reassured that they could have one. Although they benefitted from the contact, touch did not seem to create a bond between us as it had with Chris and Jonathan. While they verbally acknowledged our parenthood and sought attention constantly, they continued to refuse both our authority and our love.

Thomas and I finally reached a deeper level of closeness, following an absolutely horrible confrontation. After almost two and a half years of rebellion, Thomas had continued to ignore our direction and was in trouble for some major incident almost on a daily basis. Jim and I had tried every form of discipline we knew, with no indication that Thomas would ever change his ways.

Finally, determined that Thomas should not end up in juvenile detention, I set up a juvenile boot camp at home. When Thomas was not in school, he was working. He carried the wood from trees that Jim had split for firewood, he pulled weeds, he cleaned house. When we ran out of chores, he stood next to me and did exercises, rotating among sit-ups, push-ups, jumping jacks, and deep-knee bends. He was given rest periods when he simply stood. Jim was skeptical of the whole thing.

The first two days, Thomas yelled the whole time he worked. He hated us; he hated this family; the only reason we had adopted him was to work him to death. But by the end of his week at boot camp, Thomas was so exhausted and sore that he simply cried. The last day, all of his defenses were worn down, and we talked about the fact that he didn't like what had happened to him in his life, but that we loved him and that he would remain a member of this family. He was too tired to respond.

I went to bed praying that our son would somehow come around. I was not sure what difference to expect the next morning, but Thomas came downstairs cheerful and ready to enjoy a day free of hard labor. His attitude improved dramatically and consistently over the next several weeks. He began to emulate Jim's actions and to cooperate with his siblings. He quit fighting about his homework and chores every day. He wanted to be our son, and he wanted us to like him. I do not know exactly what happened. Maybe the technique was terrific; maybe the timing was right; maybe the good Lord took pity on our son (or on us). Whatever it was, it worked, and I am thankful each day for the changes it brought.

I cannot say that one particular incident or sequence of events has created a bond between my daughter and me. It has been a slow and faltering process. Recognizing that we had little in common at the start, I made deliberate attempts to bond. One such time, for example, I agreed to her request that we both should get our ears pierced. Two years later, I had pierced ears, which for 36 years I had lived without,

and my daughter's ears had grown back together after con-
stant battles and two major infections. Slowly, we continue to
build a history of daily activities and memories that draws
us closer together over time.

That's the Breaks

I was across campus when the call came to my office. The
message was sitting on my desk when I returned. "Betty fell
and broke her arm. Call Tom as soon as possible," a colleague
had scribbled on a scrap of paper.

At first, I wasn't particularly alarmed. After all, just a
couple of months earlier I had received a similar call from
Betty's school.

"Betty fell and hurt her arm," the secretary had relayed. "I
think it's broken."

I had hastily left work, picked up my moaning daughter,
and rushed her to the clinic. There, the doctors carefully
removed the makeshift splint the school staff had applied, and
thoroughly examined Betty's arm. Fortunately, her arm was
not broken. It wasn't even sprained. Relieved, but a little
irritated, I took my actress daughter home.

Initially, this latest incident appeared no different. When
I called the day camp, Tom informed me that Betty had fallen
off the jungle gym and hurt her arm. Thinking it might be
broken, and unable to reach me, he had called an ambulance.
Betty was currently enroute to a hospital in downtown Atlanta.

I quickly notified Darlene, then headed to the hospital.
Betty was sitting in a wheelchair when I arrived. "Dad, I broke
my arm," she groaned.

"Again?" I quipped. "You just broke it two months ago."

Betty rolled her eyes at me, then winced at the floor. She was obviously in pain. Concerned, but unconvinced, I offered what sympathy and support I could.

Soon we headed upstairs for a series of x-rays. Then we waited impatiently for the results. After what seemed like hours, the technician finally approached us, nodding her head ominously.

"She has definitely broken her arm — about two inches below the shoulder," the technician informed me. "But, that's not what we're concerned about," she continued. "We think she also fractured her elbow. We have to take more x-rays."

With mixed emotions, I realized my daughter was not acting this time. The next set of x-rays confirmed earlier suspicions. Betty had suffered a nasty compound fracture to her elbow. "Dad, I *told* you I broke my arm," she stated flatly.

I held her quivering body while the doctor forced the pieces of Betty's elbow back into their proper places. "Daddy, it hurts so bad," she cried.

"I know, Honey....I know," I soothed.

Darlene relieved me later that evening. She slept in a chair next to Betty's bed that night. Our daughter would not be left alone in a strange, scary place, she informed me.

Before I left, I gazed upon the now-silent form of my sleeping daughter. Betty had truly needed us, and really appreciated us being there. For our part, Darlene and I were very thankful that we were available for this little person in her time of need. *That's what parents are for*, I thought to myself.

Every cloud has a silver lining, and it didn't take long to find this one. Over the next two months, the three boys made Betty's bed, fetched pillows for her arm, took turns playing with her, and cared for her constantly. They showed genuine love and compassion for their injured sibling. Indeed, more bonding took place in those two months than in the previous year and a half. As Betty's bones grew together, so too did our family.

Through Their Eyes

As Darlene and I were preparing this chapter, we asked our children to recall some of their memories concerning adoption. Each child's unique perspective hinted at more profound issues which will color their lives in the years ahead. Here, in their own words, is what they had to say:

Christopher (age 12)

"All adopted kids have one thing in common: that there is someone who cares enough to bring them into their home and give them food, shelter, and love.

"I would say the first six months were about the hardest months out of my life so far. Me being 5 and my brother Jonathan being 4 entered the lives of the now-called 'mom and dad.' These months were filled with fits, crying, yelling, and in-the-corner sessions. It's hard to explain, so imagine yourself starting your whole life over. You have a new home, new parents, new toys. To all the kids who may be feeling down, here's some advice: learn the rules of your new house and family. Live and survive at least the first year. Make a good impression on your new parents. Do as you are told. Don't lie but tell the truth.

"Rules, punishments, rewards, and allowances: these all

fall under the word 'home.' First on our list is rules, meaning that you have to follow some said commandments. Next on our list is punishment. This is something that happens if the household rules aren't followed. Moving on we find the word 'reward.' This is something that is given or said when you follow directions or rules. And last, but not least, on our list is allowances. If the word money means anything to you, behave and make sure you get your weekly allowance."

Chris has always been a "thinker." He carefully analyzes and assesses every new situation, weighing the cost and benefit of each action. Artistic and creative, Chris enjoys leading others and helping them solve problems. For example, he once opened a small store to help Betty learn the concept of money. Chris likes to invent things, from new recipes to new tools.

Jonathan (age 11)

"When I was being adopted, I did not know what was happening at all. I did not know what they would look like, how they would act, or how they would treat me. So, I thought they would be nice, and I was right. When I got there, the house looked like a mansion. I think I fitted in just right. My feelings have not changed.

"When I had a new brother and sister come into the family, it was very different. At first, it was all going wrong. They started out as mean, little brats. They were difficult to get along with. They always hit people and lied. At times my brother would yell from the yard that he was going to kill me. And at times my sister would try to break down her door.

"At times I did not like them and got scared of them, but at times I enjoyed being around them. When I did not like them, it was because they had bad temper tantrums that were a super mess. They hit, kicked, spit, threw things, yelled, and punched. They did not know the rules. Here are two things I remember most: Betty throwing stuff at Dad, and Thomas screaming in the yard he was going to kill me.

"I think that my brother and sister had a lot of bad things happen in their other families. They had to be taken from one family to another. That is what probably made them have bad habits — because of what their parents did. That is what they copied and that is what they did. But, now they have got all those habits over with, with the help of mom and dad. They have solved all the problems.

"I sometimes think I am the peacemaker, or the person who solves the problems. The others seem to start, or stay out of, everything. I think it is nice for people to adopt kids. I am glad I was adopted. I think I am lucky to have nice parents who care for me. I hope other kids have a nice ending like mine."

Jonathan is indeed a peacemaker. He rushes to aid the underdog in a fight and argues vehemently against perceived injustices to others. Jonathan is extremely generous with his money, and generally is the child most willing to help with special chores and projects. He possesses a great sense of humor, easily makes friends, and is becoming a skilled musician.

Betty (age 12)

"When I first came here, I felt discouraged for awhile. I misbehaved by throwing toys, shoes, anything I could at my parents. I used to scratch, bite, spit, slap, and kick at my parents when I got mad. I told lies, kicked the wall, and screamed at the top of my lungs. I hit other people and started fights. I was not a calm child. After awhile, I started to settle down.

"When I first came, it was a hard time for me. I had to get in shape because I was a fat kid when I came. I did not like working out. I wanted to eat and watch television.

"I was a little scared to come here because at first I thought it was going to be a bad home and I didn't know what to expect. I thought I was going to get away with stuff when I came here...at my other houses I got away with stuff. I felt happy to have two new brothers because the other brothers I had were pains-in-the-rear. Going to a new school made me discouraged because I thought I was not going to make any friends. I still miss my real mom.

"It made me feel unhappy when people started to say things about me. Like, for example: 'How can you stand her? She is a pain-in-the-neck.' I started to feel that nobody loved me anymore.

"My feelings now are happy because I have never really had a family that cared, loved, and respected one another. The other house which I went to were some adults that wanted children but did not know how to take care of children. They wanted to be my adopted parents, but they had no way of knowing how to take care of kids. My feelings about living here are happy because I have parents that know how to be parents and it is a very nice family to be in. I think I will always fit in a family that cares, loves, respects, and treats one another like you want to be treated."

Betty is gregarious, and she truly values her many friendships. She is also a caregiver, giving of herself to neighbors, animals, anyone or anything that needs assistance. She frequently includes special requests for others in her prayers. No longer "fat," Betty has become the most athletic member of our family.

Thomas (age 10)

"Adoption means they can take care of me and give me a place to sleep and a roof to lie under. That is what it means to me.

"It was hard to come from one family to another family. You have new brothers and you do not know what to be. If the children at your new school laugh at you, just ignore them. At first I did not know how to talk properly. Now I am on level.

"It was hard to come to a new mom and dad because they did not do things my own mother and father did. I used to not have chores because my own mom and dad did not give me chores. Here we share chores like who sets the table, who dusts, who sweeps the floors, and who cleans the bathrooms. I feed both cats. We are still doing the sharing.

"I am glad I live in a good family. We all go on bike rides and we ride a go-cart. It is fun staying with my family. I came here when I was 7 years old, and now I am 10 years old. I feel it has been a good 3 years. Now I live happily ever after."

Thomas is a perfectionist. He has the neatest handwriting in the world, and takes considerable pride in a job well done. Though he is usually very serious, Thomas shows all the signs of becoming a practical joker. In the past few months alone, he has scared his mother half to death by jumping out from behind doors, made a birthday card for Jonathan with nothing written in it, and informed me that babies come from boys (which had me rather concerned until he couldn't contain his laughter any longer).

Time Heals All Things

A single court procedure creates the legal bond called adoption, but it is the process of learning to live with and to love one another that adoption is all about. Since we first adopted, crisis has followed crisis. We ranked high on the stress-test-of-life-changes scale for several years in a row. We experienced personal stress, relationship stress, financial stress, career stress, physical stress, and never-enough-time stress....and through sharing these experiences, we have grown into a family.

At first, it was like squeezing square pegs into round holes. The children didn't fit into our well-ordered lives, and we didn't fit their idea of parents. Our idealism faded as we were forced to examine our lives in excruciating detail. One by one, each person's beliefs and actions were challenged, weighed, and then either reinforced or discarded as we defined our family relationships. In some ways, we changed our children; and in just as many ways, they changed us.

What helped us through all of this turmoil? Looking back, we have been able to identify several keys to success. Persistence (sometimes sheer stubbornness) helped considerably. We were committed to making this adoption thing work and would not give up. The experience gained through our first adoption helped us the second time around. Our expectations and techniques did change through trial, however, and flexibility in our approach was often necessary.

Balance was important. We tried to balance our plan to integrate the children into our lifestyle with their desire to make us into the type of parents they each wanted; we weighed the needs of each child against the sometimes conflicting needs of the others and of ourselves as parents.

Our children's early experiences with birth parents, foster families, and previous adoption attempts definitely influenced who they are and what they expect from life. Our role as parents included helping our children shift their focus from a reaction to the circumstances of their pasts (Where did I come from?) to seeing choices for their futures (Where am I going?). Finding a balance between these two questions is an on-going exercise requiring lengthy and constant discussions.

The simple passage of time helped to slowly build a new library of thoughts and feelings in our children's minds. Our daily routines, repeated over and over, eventually gained enough strength through practice to offset earlier experiences. Past events will someday be remembered and understood in a new light by a child who has matured with other experiences.

We have come to think of our role in parenting as that of a butterfly's chrysalis. Our children were not born to us; they do not carry our genes. They lived their early years in an uncertain environment, growing and surviving as best they could. Now, we surround them with our love and protection as they develop to their full potential. Someday, we will release them into the world, with the strength and energy to fly.

Epilogue

It has been over seven years since Darlene and I adopted Christopher and Jonathan, and over three years since we adopted Betty and Thomas. From the day our children first walked through our door, we have not been the same. Our lives were truly changed for the better. Rarely does a day pass that I don't thank God for leading my steps (perhaps pushing at times) down the path to adoption.

Darlene and I dearly love our children. We truly enjoy being their parents and are so happy to be a part of their lives. It's difficult to imagine life without them.

Was it worth all the early — and sometimes lengthy — trials and tribulations? Absolutely! Would we go through it all again? Certainly.

If you know someone who has recently adopted an older child, we hope this book helps you better understand what that family may be experiencing and how you might better offer your friendship and support during the difficult days ahead. Be slow to judge but quick to encourage. That's what friends are for.

If you are in the process of adopting an older child, we hope our story offers you encouragement and support. Yes, the road will be rough at times, but you *will* survive. And rest assured: there *are* others who *do* understand what you and your family are going through.

Lastly, if you are thinking about adding to your family through adoption, we hope you will consider adopting older children. There are still many awaiting their chance at a permanent home and their *forever parents*.

Order Form

Please send __ copies of *Forever Parents: Adopting Older Children.* I have enclosed a check or money order for $11.95 per book, plus a $2.00 shipping charge.

Name: _____

Address: _____

City: _____

State: _____ Zip Code: _____

Mail to: Adele Enterprises
PO Box 553
Union City, GA 30291-0553

Thank you for your order!